Teaching
CIVICS TODAY

The iCivics Approach to
Classroom Innovation and Student Engagement

John Larmer, M.A.Ed.

Contributing Author

Jennifer L. Prior, Ph.D.

iCivics Consultants

Emma Humphries, Ph.D.
Chief Education Officer and Deputy Director of CivXNow
Taylor Davis, M.T.
Director of Curriculum and Content
Natacha Scott, MAT
Director of Educator Engagement
David Buchanan, M.A.Ed.
Director of Massachusetts Programs

Publishing Credits

Corinne Burton, M.A.Ed., *Publisher*
Aubrie Nielsen, M.S.Ed., *EVP of Content Development*
Véronique Bos, *Creative Director*
Cathy Hernandez, *Senior Content Manager*
Fabiola Sepulveda, *Jr. Art Director*
Rachel Berg Scherer, M.A.Ed., *Editor*
David Slayton, *Assistant Editor*

Image Credits

p. 83 left Library of Congress [LC-USZC2-1058]; p. 83 right Library of Congress [91898263]; all other images from iStock and/or Shutterstock

A division of Teacher Created Materials
5482 Argosy Avenue
Huntington Beach, CA 92649-1039
www.tcmpub.com/shell-education
ISBN 978-1-0876-5018-0
© 2022 Shell Educational Publishing, Inc.
Printed in USA. WOR004
The name "iCivics" and the iCivics logo are
registered trademarks of iCivics, Inc.

Table of Contents

Table of Contents *(cont.)*

Foreword

Teaching civics today is not what it was 100, 50, or even 10 years ago. We have come a long way from the dry textbooks and boring diagrams that so many associate with their own civics classes. We have also come a long way from the singular-perspective narratives that filled those instructional materials.

If your civics or government textbook had a picture of the Supreme Court Justices, it likely was not a model of representation. Indeed, for much of U.S. history, it was difficult for many Americans to see themselves reflected in the Court. But as representation has grown in government, so too has it grown in the instructional materials we use to teach our young people about our nation's institutions of government.

Another notable difference from "your grandmother's civics class" is the variety of teaching strategies and the level of engagement offered within these strategies. Stand-and-deliver lectures have been replaced with simulations and classroom discussions of current and controversial topics. The old standby of "read the chapter and answer the questions at the end" has been replaced with authentic inquiries and relevant project-based learning. This book contains clear and practical descriptions of these approaches, as well as helpful suggestions for implementing them in your classroom.

It's not just the perspectives and pedagogy that have evolved over time—so too has the attention civics has received, the frameworks that drive its teaching, and the sociopolitical climate in which it is taught. As a former classroom teacher and a historian of education, I have both experienced and studied the evolution of civic education in the United States. I am happy to report that, after years of neglect, civics is experiencing a resurgence in interest, prioritization, and efforts to ensure we're teaching it in the best way possible. From the C3 framework to the Educating for American Democracy initiative, we now have so much more thoughtful and realistic guidance to ensure deep and engaging civic learning for today's students. You will find uncomplicated and accessible descriptions of all this and more in the following pages!

One thing that hasn't changed about teaching civics today is its enduring importance—an educated citizenry remains vital to the health of our constitutional democracy. As Thomas Jefferson so eloquently stated in an 1816 letter, "If a nation expects to be ignorant and free in a state of civilization, it expects what never was and never will be." It was for this very reason that a system of public schooling was established in the United States. For those of us who understand the unretractable link between democracy and education, preparing young people for their roles as citizens will always be the primary mission of education.

In my current role, I serve as the Chief Education Officer for iCivics, an education nonprofit reimagining civic learning for American democracy. Our founder, retired Supreme Court Justice Sandra Day O'Connor, transformed the Supreme Court and its representation when she became its first female Justice. After retirement, she transformed civic education when she founded iCivics and brought video games and other engaging instructional resources to what was then a dull and uninspired civics market.

This book reflects the pedagogical innovation Justice O'Connor brought to our field. I hope you will find it enjoyable and impactful as you join us in fulfilling what the Justice saw as her most important work: providing every student in the United States with high-quality civic education.

—Emma Humphries, Ph.D.
iCivics Chief Education Officer and
Deputy Director of CivXNow

Preface

I wrote this book because I care about helping students understand the concepts, values, and skills necessary for the United States to thrive as a democracy: participatory citizenship, respect for differences, belief in the importance of reason and evidence, being willing to compromise, and more.

There should be increased emphasis on civic education in schools, from kindergarten through 12th grade—and not just more, but better civic education. To me, that does not mean lecturing, textbooks and worksheets, and memorization of facts; it means more engaging and active teaching methods. Students should be practicing democratic values in the classroom, discussing civics-related issues, and participating as citizens of their communities and the wider world. I'm a big advocate for project-based learning, so you'll find many examples of civics projects in this book that connect to real-world issues and problems and student interests.

I hope this book helps reinforce the vital role teachers play in providing more and better civic education. If you're not already persuaded to take on this role, I hope you will be after reading this. In addition to helping to strengthen our country, teaching civics can be rewarding and downright fun. I know I enjoyed it as a high school social studies teacher. The activities and resources described in this book will help you and your students enjoy it, too.

Here's an overview of what the book covers. In Chapter 1, we explore the importance of civic education: why it is valuable and why it's needed today, more than ever. We look at why civic education has declined in recent decades and new bipartisan efforts to promote civic education.

Chapter 2 looks at what, exactly, is civic education? We consider the goals of a good civic education and what citizenship means. Then, we delve into the *College, Career, and Civic Life (C3) Framework for Social Studies State Standards* and the recent *Educating for American Democracy (EAD) Roadmap*. Finally, we explore some of the tensions and challenges in civic education and the need for "reflective patriotism."

Chapter 3 is where what I think of as the fun part begins. Here we dig into best practices in civic education. We'll examine the research about why active learning is better than memorization, and we'll look at how the C3 Framework and EAD Roadmap promote active learning and inquiry. This chapter also considers how to teach civil discourse, how to approach controversial issues, information literacy, and civics learning beyond the classroom.

Integrating literacy in civic education is the focus of Chapter 4. We'll see how English language arts standards align with best practices for teaching civics. Then, we'll delve into how to teach reading, writing, speaking, and listening in civic education and how to teach civics during literacy instruction. We've included recommendations for fiction and nonfiction that teaches students about civics.

Chapter 5 is rich with time-tested strategies, ideas, and resources for teaching the dispositions and skills that are part of civic education. We'll consider how to practice democracy in your classroom, why and how to teach public speaking, best practices for teaching content, including using simulations and experiential learning, and current events. We'll also look at project-based learning: what it is and is not, and see well-developed examples of civics projects.

As you can tell, there's a lot in here. You'll also find links to helpful resources and additional information to explore—it can be quite a rabbit hole, so we've carefully curated it all. Other resources from Teacher Created Materials and iCivics will help you on your mission, too, so I encourage you to check them out.

Best wishes for your teaching, and may your students be the citizens our nation needs!

Chapter 1

Why Is Civic Education Important Today?

Before we get into the serious and potentially thorny issues around civics, let's start by saying this: it's fun to teach! You might already have felt the rewards that come from awakening young minds to concepts such as liberty, justice, and responsibility. You might have had the experience of seeing your students get charged up about a mock election in their school, a role-play activity about the American Revolution, or a project in which they tackled a real-world problem in their community. It's exciting to see students actively engaged in their learning and to see them becoming the kinds of citizens we need today. If you have not taught civics before, we trust you, too, will find it rewarding.

We hope you are ready to think about why and how civics should be taught today and to deepen your practice by learning about some strategies and resources. Now, on to the serious question of why civic education is important today.

The Need for Civic Education

This country needs civic education now more than ever. The United States needs its people to value democracy and understand their role as citizens. Two modern-day U.S. presidents reminded us of the importance of democracy and our role as engaged citizens. Ronald Reagan, on the 40th anniversary of D-Day, reminded us that World War II was fought for democracy. He said, "Democracy is worth dying for, because it's the most deeply honorable form of government ever devised by man." A generation later, Barack Obama pointed out that "Democracy was never meant to be transactional—you give me your vote; I make everything better. It requires an active and informed citizenry."

However, many young people have not been given the education they need for informed, active, and healthy participation in our democracy—and that's where you come in, as a teacher. You have a vital role to play!

Research shows that students who receive quality civic education are more likely to:

★ vote

★ discuss politics at home

★ complete college

★ develop skills that lead to employment

★ give back to their communities through volunteering and working on community issues

★ be more confident in their ability to speak publicly and communicate with their elected representatives (Levine and Kawashima-Ginsberg 2017)

Meeting Challenges Together

We face challenges today that we must meet together. Yet, in the last few decades, we have felt more divided than we used to. Many people have lost faith in government and do not understand the democratic processes. The institutions that used to bring communities together have been in decline. Many people feel powerless, apathetic, and cynical.

Recent events in our country highlight the need for better civic education. Although the 2020 election saw an increase in voter participation, it also brought a rise in misinformation and doubt about the validity of the results.

As we approach the 250th anniversary of the founding of the nation, "We the People" must repair the foundations of our republic. To find our way forward, what we need more than ever is "reflective patriotism," described as "love of country with clear-eyed wisdom about our successes and failures" (Educating for American Democracy 2021a, 8). The process of developing reflective patriotism is fostered in schools in addition to in homes.

Patriotism can also be thought of as a love of a country's ideals—even if not fully realized—and a hope for its future potential. Accordingly, civic education can frame "citizenship" in terms of being a member of a community and caring about others, while still considering what it means to be a citizen of the nation.

A Look at Long-Term Trends

It may not be surprising that many Americans do not know history well, and a high number do not participate in elections, politics, and civic life. Students typically rank social studies low on the list of school subjects that interest them. This has been true for a long time: an internet search of "why kids don't like social studies" will take you to an article with that exact title from 1982. Research dating back to the 1960s shows that many students from elementary to high school find social studies to be boring and not relevant to their lives.

Students' Lack of Knowledge about Civics

Scores in civics for fourth and eighth graders on the National Assessment of Educational Progress (NAEP) improved slightly between 1998 and 2014, but they still have a ways to go (The Nation's Report Card, n.d.). The scores for 2018 were not significantly different from 2014: only 23 percent scored at or above the "proficient" level. The gains since 1998 were mostly due to the improvement in scores for lower-performing students; the scores for middle- and higher-performing students were unchanged.

The scores for 2018 showed:

- ★ 27 percent of students scored at the "below basic" level
- ★ 49 percent of students scored at the "basic" level
- ★ 21 percent of students scored at the "proficient" level
- ★ 2 percent of students scored at the "advanced" level

To give a sense of what achievement on the NAEP test means, the three levels of performance for eighth graders are:

1. Students at the "basic" level could identify that the right of free assembly was being exercised when looking at a photograph of the 1963 March on Washington.

2. Students at the "proficient" level could explain how public protests can achieve political goals.

3. Students at the "advanced" level could evaluate how a quotation about criticizing the government could be an expression of patriotism.

The NAEP civics test scores tell us something more. There is a growing "civic education gap" along class and racial lines, which we will discuss later.

Young People's Mixed Support for Democracy

Like many adults today, young people also have rising doubts about democracy. A 2020 report states, "We find that across the globe, younger generations have become steadily more dissatisfied with democracy—not only in absolute terms, but also relative to older cohorts at comparable stages of life" (Foa et al. 2020).

There is also evidence of a rising hostility to core democratic ideals, such as compromise and accepting political opponents as legitimate. More young people today—not just in the United States but around the world—are finding a "populist" approach to democracy appealing. The same report explains the implications of such an approach:

> A defining feature of populism is its 'anti-pluralism,' in that rather than seeing society as a wide spectrum of competing viewpoints and interests, to be sifted through elections, representative institutions, and the slow churn of the policymaking process, populists instead portray society as divisible into two camps: good against bad, the 'pure' versus the deplorable. Such an approach is fundamentally in conflict with the foundational principle of democratic politics, which requires partisans to accept their opponents' equal dignity and moral worth, and by consequence, their equal right to express their viewpoints, organize, and contest public office. (Foa et al. 2020, 23)

Americans' Participation and Belief in Democracy

According to Gallup polls conducted since 1973, Americans' distrust in the federal government has been growing, along with distrust of other institutions, such as public schools, organized religion, banks, big business, organized labor, and the media. A 2018 survey found only 18 percent of Americans trusted the government.

Americans do not even trust fellow citizens. In a 2017 survey, only 33 percent of Americans said they have a "good deal of confidence in the wisdom of the American people when it comes to making political decisions," compared to 57 percent in 2007 and 64 percent in 1997. An increasingly large number of Americans not only disagree with but also dislike people who support a different political party (Levine and Kawashima-Ginsberg 2017).

Along with growing mistrust, Americans' civic knowledge and public engagement are also at historic lows. A 2016 survey, for example, found only 26 percent of Americans can name all three branches of the government—a big decline from previous years—and 31 percent could not name any. This is not a trivial fact; if people do not know the three branches of government, they cannot understand the fundamental importance of checks and balances and an independent judiciary in a democracy.

Low voter turnout is another indicator of lack of engagement. The United States lags behind most other democracies around the world in voting rates. In the 2016 presidential election, almost 56 percent of the voting-age population voted, which placed the United States 13th out of 35 nations. More people than ever before voted in the 2020 presidential election, but a record-breaking voter turnout was still just 67 percent of the population.

Decline in Civic Life

Another development in recent decades has weakened democracy and caused Americans to trust one another less: we don't get together with other people as much as we used to. In most of American history, people engaged in large civic associations, such as religious congregations, labor unions, and clubs. Participation in these groups has dropped in recent decades. So has the readership for daily local newspapers, another way we connect with our communities.

In his 2001 book *Bowling Alone: The Collapse and Revival of American Community*, Robert Putnam captured the problem. His driving metaphor is based on the fact that thousands of Americans used to belong to bowling leagues but do not anymore:

> Television, two-career families, suburban sprawl, generational changes in values—these and other changes in American society have meant that fewer and fewer of us find that the League of Women Voters, or the United Way, or the Shriners, or the monthly bridge club, or even a Sunday picnic with friends fits the way we have come to live. Our growing social-capital deficit threatens educational performance, safe neighborhoods, equitable tax collection, democratic responsiveness, everyday honesty, and even our health and happiness. (Putnam 2001, 267)

Today, of course, the internet is another contributing factor Putnam would put on the list. While people do form associations online, they tend to be narrower groups of like-minded individuals. And when you're interacting face-to-face with someone, as opposed to online, it's not so easy to disagree disrespectfully or dismiss them entirely.

Alexis de Tocqueville, the French observer who famously traveled the United States in the 1830s and wrote *Democracy in America*, thought Americans' habit of joining associations was key to the success of its democracy. In such associations, Americans learned how to talk civilly with one another, exchange ideas, and make decisions through compromise and consensus.

There is also a troubling equity angle to the decline in joining associations. Working class Americans are especially less engaged than they were 50 years ago. More and more young people report living in what's called a "civic desert," where they have no or few chances to meet, discuss issues, or address problems. This is true for 60 percent of rural young people and about 30 percent of urban and suburban residents. Low-income youth of all backgrounds report feeling especially disconnected from civic life (Putnam 2001).

The State of Civic Education

Civic education is tied closely to history education, and both have been neglected in recent years. This is not to say there aren't dedicated teachers who want to prepare and motivate students for participation in civic life. There are many great programs available for both classroom use and as extracurricular opportunities for interested students. Rather, attention and time devoted to teaching social studies in general has dropped.

One might assume this is because the No Child Left Behind Act of 2002 only tested literacy and math. The same was true for the Race to the Top grants of 2009. These federal policies have certainly been factors, but the amount of time devoted to social studies in U.S. elementary schools was small even before that: below 10 percent of total instructional time in the 1980s and 1990s. So, it's more complicated than just the effect of federal legislation.

The teaching of civics and history has declined in the United States for several reasons:

1. A priority on literacy and mathematics

2. Lack of testing

3. Attention to STEAM

4. Teachers stretched thin, with a lack of high-quality materials and training

5. Controversy over content

Let's look at each one more closely.

A Priority on Literacy and Mathematics

Literacy and mathematics are rightfully seen as fundamental "gatekeeper" skills, so more time has been devoted to those subjects in the elementary school day and week. This is where the influence of No Child Left Behind is most felt in other disciplines. There was a drop beginning in 2002, as shown in Figure 1.1.

Figure 1.1—Time Spent Per Subject in U.S. Public Schools, Grades 1–4

Subject Area	Average number of hours per week		Percentage of student school week	
	1999–2000	2007–2008	1999–2000	2007–2008
English Language Arts	10.9	11.7	33.6	35.6
Mathematics	5.7	5.6	17.4	16.9
Science	2.6	2.3	8.1	7.1
Social Studies	2.9	2.3	8.9	7.1

Source: National Center for Education Statistics, n.d., 2015–2016

Even in middle school, students spend less time in social studies classes than they do in English language arts (ELA), math, or science, as shown in Figure 1.2.

Figure 1.2—Time Spent Per Subject in U.S. Public Schools, Grade 8, 2011–2012

Subject Area	Average number of hours per week	Percentage of student school week
English Language Arts	6.5	19.4
Mathematics	5.0	14.8
Science	4.3	12.7
Social Studies	4.2	12.5

(Hoyer and Sparks 2017)

We are not advocating for equal time for all subjects. If students need to read better, they should receive more reading instruction, since it's an essential skill not only for all academic subjects but also for future educational opportunity and for life in general. The same is true for math. Science, the arts, and physical education deserve time, too. But this country also needs more and better civic education.

There is a particular problem, however, with how students are being taught to read, and it connects to the teaching of social studies. Most literacy programs today teach reading by emphasizing general reading skills. A literacy program does need to teach reading skills, but it cannot be devoid of academic content.

A recent study supports this argument. Researchers followed the progress of thousands of students from kindergarten to fifth grade. They looked at the amount of classroom time spent on different subjects and whether students who spend more time on certain subjects make greater progress in reading. They also considered how these effects differ by student characteristics. Researchers found:

★ Elementary school students in the United States spend much more time on ELA than on any other subject.

★ Increased instructional time in social studies—an additional 30 minutes per day—is associated with improved reading ability. Increased time in ELA or other subjects did not have this effect.

★ The students who benefit the most from additional social studies time are girls and those from lower-income and/or non-English-speaking homes. (Tyner and Kabourek 2020)

We will discuss later how to teach civics in ways that build literacy and how to teach literacy in ways that build knowledge of civics and history.

Lack of Testing

High-stakes standardized tests in most states do not include social studies, and as the saying goes, "What gets tested gets taught."

The current federal law governing education, the Every Student Succeeds Act, replaced No Child Left Behind in 2015. It reduces the amount of testing for ELA and math and requires a science assessment, but it does not include a requirement to test social studies. As of 2018, only 21 states tested students in history, government/civics, or economics. Only eight states require students to take the U.S. citizenship test.

Even when history and civics are tested, the tests are not "high stakes" for teachers and schools to the same degree that reading and math test scores are (Railey and Brennan 2016).

The results of reading and math tests get much more attention from schools, the media, and the public, and teacher accountability systems typically do not include test scores for social studies.

Attention to STEM

The STEM subjects (science, technology, engineering, and math) are seen as a pathway to college and careers in the modern economy. Accordingly, they've gotten a lot of attention from educators, governments, and curriculum providers. Interest in promoting STEM has also been driven by our nation's desire to remain competitive in a global economy. The increased emphasis on math and science traces back to the Cold War in the late 1950s, when the United States was competing against the Soviet Union for technological dominance.

Much less money is now spent on history and civic education than on STEM subjects. In the early 2000s, for example, the federal government used to spend about $40 million a year on civics programs. In the decade since 2010, it has spent about $4 million a year, compared to $3 billion a year on STEM. And beginning around 2012, the time spent on science exceeded that spent on social studies in grades 1–4.

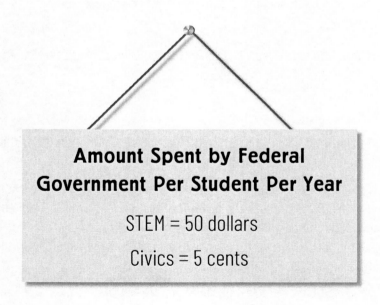

Amount Spent by Federal Government Per Student Per Year

STEM = 50 dollars

Civics = 5 cents

Teachers Stretched Thin and Inadequate Resources

Social studies as a subject area includes several other subject areas. In addition to U.S. history and civics, it also encompasses world history, world cultures, geography, and economics. High schools also offer courses in psychology, anthropology, religious studies, sociology, and more. Consequently, a social studies teacher is often a "jack of all trades." At the same time, federal, state, and local governments, plus funders and curriculum providers, have other priorities. As such, they have not provided teachers with the high-quality materials or training they need.

These four factors combine to create a perfect storm of neglect for history and civics. Samantha Stearns, an eighth grade social studies teacher, noted that this means elementary and intermediate school teachers are tasked not only with teaching multiple content areas but also with increasing standardized test scores in reading and math. Teachers subsequently integrate social studies instruction into other disciplines, such as using a story about the American Revolution as a backdrop for a reading lesson. But she notes why this is problematic:

> On paper, the student has received social studies 'minutes' as mandated by the state or district, but in reality, the student has learned about an event, a person, or a place without any historical context. The student, therefore, views the topic in isolation, never to be thought about again. Young learners' inherent curiosity is stifled when they can't move beyond the *what* to also explore the *why* and *how*: the very essence of what quality social studies education should encourage. (Stearns 2019, para. 4)

Controversy over Content

Unlike STEM, it is difficult—if not impossible—in this era of political polarization for experts in the field of history and civics to reach consensus about what should be taught in schools. This means history and civics have not been included in the major efforts to reform education, from No Child Left Behind to various state-level efforts.

This is also nothing new in America; disagreement about our history goes back at least to the Civil War. An attempt to set national standards for teaching history in the 1990s was abandoned after generating too much controversy. The tension continues today, as we debate the history and legacy of marginalized groups in American history.

We can take an approach to civic education that will help the situation. The *Excellence in History and Civics for All Learners* report from Educating for American Democracy showcases the need to disagree productively:

> Fraught though the terrain is, America urgently needs a shared, national conversation about what is most important to teach in American history and civics, how to teach it, and above all, why. We believe there is a way forward if we can build a national conversation that is at once ideologically pluralist, grounded in classroom experience, and accessible both to teachers of all backgrounds and to diverse student learners. (2021a, 10)

Inequitable Access and Achievement

Another highly important reason to revitalize civic education has to do with equity. For our democracy to be healthy and inclusive, all young people must be given the knowledge, skills, and equal opportunity not only to participate but also to become civic and political leaders. Without that, substantial numbers of people will be left out of civic and political life, which ultimately leads to discontent and dysfunction.

The "crowding out" effect of emphasizing reading and math in school to the detriment of social studies has been particularly felt by low-income students, especially students of color. Lower-performing schools enrolling higher percentages of disadvantaged students typically focus their energy on raising test scores in reading and math, not civics.

The NAEP test reflects disparities in civic education. Comparative results from 1998–2018 increasingly show white and/or affluent students scoring higher than low-income and/or minority students (Hansen et al. 2020). Differences in reading and math scores, on the other hand, have decreased. Researcher (and former middle school teacher) Meira Levinson has called this a "civic empowerment gap" (2010).

One More Reason

There is an additional argument for more and better civic education. Students as young as those in elementary school are well aware of current issues that need to be understood and addressed. They've heard about and seen—and sometimes joined—efforts to do something about societal problems. To understand these problems and contribute to their solutions, students need to learn civics and history. The motivation is there; we just need to capitalize on it.

New Efforts to Promote Civic Education

The National Endowment for the Humanities and the U.S. Department of Education recently launched an effort to revitalize education in civics and history in the United States. A diverse and cross-ideological group of experts and educators published the Educating for American Democracy Report and accompanying Roadmap in March 2021. These publications describe the role of civic education to equip "members of a democratic society to understand, appreciate, nurture, and—where necessary—improve their political system and civil society." The report goes on to explain, "The word 'civic' denotes the virtues, assets, and activities that a free people need to govern themselves well. When civic education succeeds, all people are prepared and motivated to participate effectively in civic life" (Educating for American Democracy 2021a, 9).

Also in March 2021, a bipartisan group of senators introduced a bill to support and expand access to civics and history education. The "Civics Secures Democracy Act" would provide grants to states, nonprofits, institutions of higher education, and civic education researchers and support teacher professional development programs. The legislation does not propose to develop any national curriculum, as that's left up to states and local school districts. In explaining its purpose, the bill states, "In today's contentious civil environment, it is more important than ever that students are equipped with knowledge of our institutions and confronted with the enduring questions of civic life and political change" (Health, Education, Labor, and Pensions, and Coons 2021).

At the time of this writing, the bill has not passed and has generated lots of debate. But whatever its ultimate fate, it shows that concern over civic education reaches through all levels of society today.

> ## The Struggle over Civics in These Times
>
> Civics is at the heart of the struggle to define the
> meaning of the American idea.... Teaching civics
> could restore health to American democracy,
> or inflame our mutual antagonisms. Events are
> currently pushing in both directions.
>
> —George Packer, Journalist and Author (2021)

The Path Forward

All of this might make you feel the importance of the mission you've been given as a teacher, right? You are not alone in this work. You'll find support as you connect with others, and this book is designed to help you along the way.

Imagine your students learning what it means to be good citizens in a democracy: how to speak and listen respectfully; how to back up their ideas with evidence from trustworthy sources; how to recognize what their local, state, and national governments do and how they can be a part of them; what the right to vote means; the importance of the rights to free speech and equal opportunity. With you as their teacher, a good civic education will prepare them to join their communities and their nation, to help make it a "more perfect union."

Restoring faith in democracy is a complex and long-term challenge facing the country. More and better civic education will not be the only solution, but it's an important part of it. In the next chapter, we'll talk more about what a good civic education in kindergarten through grade eight should include.

Reflect and Apply

1. Has your own civic engagement waned over time? Or has it increased? What outside factors have influenced it?

2. How has your time in the classroom affected your civic engagement?

3. How can you incorporate practical application in your classroom in a way that teaches students—without imparting political viewpoints upon them—how to use civic knowledge? Consider the climates of both your school and your larger community.

Chapter 2

What Is Civic Education?

The father of an elementary student in New York recently observed what his son was learning in social studies:

> By age ten he had studied the civilizations of ancient China, Africa, the early Dutch in New Amsterdam, and the Mayans. He learned about the genocide of Native Americans and slavery. But he was never taught about the founding of the republic. He didn't learn that conflicting values and practical compromises are the lifeblood of self-government. He was given no context for the meaning of freedom of expression, no knowledge of the democratic ideas that...(are threatened today)...or of the instruments with which citizens could hold those in power accountable. Our son knew about the worst betrayals of democracy...but he wasn't taught the principles that had been betrayed. He got his civics from *Hamilton*. (Packer 2019, para. 81)

This kind of social studies curriculum is common. But many parents would agree that a social studies program should also teach basic knowledge of civics and government, with a patriotic view of America.

Your own approach to civics is something you as a teacher need to decide, given your personal views and your knowledge of your school and community. This book advocates for the teaching of civics that includes basic knowledge and understanding of the ideals upon which this country was founded as well as reflection about how our country could be made better. And we agree that it's more important than ever to learn the principles of democracy. We also favor instruction that features active learning, which we will discuss more in the next chapter.

What Is a Good Civic Education?

Simply put, civic education prepares young people to be active citizens in a democracy, not just passive citizens who follow the laws, pay their taxes, and generally get along with other people. Active citizens are those who stay informed, vote, and participate in political life or the life of their communities. They may even take action to strengthen the democracy or solve problems in communities and the nation.

To develop active citizens, a good civic education should include four basic goals:

1. Instill democratic values and develop character traits for citizenship
2. Build knowledge of government and civic institutions
3. Build skills for active citizenship, such as critical thinking, how to discuss issues with others, and how to evaluate sources of information
4. Encourage and develop skills for taking action to improve our country

What Does "Citizenship" Mean?

Legally speaking, a citizen of the United States is anyone born on its soil or born of a citizen, or anyone who has become a naturalized citizen. More broadly speaking, anyone living in the United States and participating in its economic, political, and social life can show "good citizenship." When someone joins with others to help people in their community, for example, they are showing good citizenship. Peter Levine (2014) defines a citizen as anyone who seriously asks, "What should we do?" instead of asking, "What should be done?"

There has long been a debate about what kind of citizenship is best for a democracy. Joel Westheimer and Joseph Kahne (2004) categorize citizens in a democracy into three groups:

1. **Personally responsible citizen**
   - ★ Acts responsibly in their community
   - ★ Works and pays taxes
   - ★ Obeys laws
   - ★ Recycles, gives blood, or does other things that show general support for their community; may volunteer to help others in times of crisis
   - ★ *Sample action:* donates to a food drive
   - ★ *Emphasis:* good character

2. **Participatory citizen**
   - ★ Votes in elections
   - ★ Active member of community or other organizations and improvement efforts
   - ★ Knows how government works
   - ★ Knows ways to accomplish collective tasks
   - ★ *Sample action:* helps organize a food drive
   - ★ *Emphasis:* active participation and leadership

3. **Justice-oriented citizen**
   - ★ Critically assesses social, political, and economic structures to see beyond surface causes
   - ★ Seeks out and addresses injustices
   - ★ Knows about democratic social movements and how to effect systemic change
   - ★ *Sample action:* explores why people are hungry and acts to solve root causes
   - ★ *Emphasis:* questioning, debating, and changing established systems

Each of these conceptions of good citizenship has implications for how schools should prepare young people. Should it be a "traditional" education about following rules, being a good person, and a commitment to core democratic values, such as liberty and freedom of speech? This includes knowing the basics of how government works, from what local, state, and federal governments do and the three branches of government to the classic "how a bill becomes a law" lessons. Or should civic education include emphasis on civic participation or even taking action to change things?

Good civic education should include some aspects of the traditional approach combined with a more interactive, advanced approach. This reflects the recommendations in many studies and reports.

> It's just critical that if we are going to survive as a nation, that all our citizens know and understand the fundamental beliefs that caused the formation of this country... So you have to start at the beginning, and that means the Declaration of Independence.
>
> —Justice Sandra Day O'Connor, U.S. Supreme Court (ret.)

Two Guides to Civic Education

With renewed attention in the last decade to civic education and the need to teach social studies in school, many groups have published ideas and guidelines for what students should learn and how civics should be taught. We will focus on two of the major guidelines: the *College, Career, and Civic Life (C3) Framework for Social Studies State Standards: Guidance for Enhancing the Rigor of K–12 Civics, Economics, Geography, and History* (C3 Framework) and the *Educating for American Democracy Roadmap* (EAD Roadmap).

Most state standards for civics and history have been criticized for being a mile wide and an inch deep. They feature long lists of events, famous people, dates, isolated concepts, and plenty of other facts. An emphasis on factual knowledge tends to lead teachers to try to "cover" as much ground as they can, which results in superficial learning. It is certainly important to have some level of factual knowledge, but students need more than that. They need to understand what each concept means, the story it tells about our country, and what their place in it is.

Both the C3 Framework and the EAD Roadmap try to correct this problem by emphasizing depth over breadth. They organize the content with major themes and questions, supported by key concepts.

The C3 Framework

Fifteen professional organizations collaborated to create the C3 Framework. Published in 2013 by the National Council for Social Studies (NCSS), it is meant to guide states as they develop their own standards, and it has been used widely in the years since its release. The C3 Framework purports to "provide guidance to states on the concepts, skills, and disciplinary tools necessary to prepare students for college, career, and civic life" (NCSS 2013, 17).

The C3 Framework emphasizes an inquiry-based approach to social studies, which means the content and instruction are organized around "big" questions, which could be posed by the teacher or students. They could investigate compelling questions such as "Was the American Revolution revolutionary?" or "How much freedom should we have?" to learn U.S. history and civics. Rather than simply memorizing basic facts about civics and history, students learn in a more rigorous and engaging process.

The Framework is organized around an "Inquiry Arc" with four "dimensions of informed inquiry in social studies":

1. Developing questions and planning inquiries

2. Applying disciplinary concepts and tools

3. Evaluating sources and using evidence

4. Communicating conclusions and taking informed action

We'll look more closely at the *how*—or what instruction looks like in an inquiry approach using these four dimensions—in the next chapter. Here, we'll look at the *what*, or the civics content outlined by the C3 Framework for Dimension 2, applying disciplinary concepts and tools.

The Framework differentiates "conceptual content" from "curricular content," explaining, "curricular content specifies the particular ideas to be taught and the grade levels at which to teach them; conceptual content is the bigger set of ideas that frame the curricular content" (NCSS 2013, 29).

The Framework gives an example: instead of identifying forms of government, students are expected to "explain the powers and limits of the three branches of government, public officials, and bureaucracies at different levels in the United States." Similarly, rather than identifying kinds of maps, students should be able to "create maps and other graphic representations of both familiar and unfamiliar places" (NCSS 2013, 29). The focus on bigger, conceptual ideas allows local and state decision makers to specify exactly what students should be taught and when.

Connecting Content Knowledge and Engagement

According to the C3 Framework, the goal of civic education is "productive civic engagement." For that to happen, students need to understand not just civic and political institutions, democratic processes, rules, and laws but also "civic virtues and democratic principles" (NCSS 2013). The Framework explains the connections between civic knowledge, virtues, and engagement and why each is important.

First, the Framework explains why basic knowledge is important: "In a constitutional democracy, productive civic engagement requires knowledge of the history, principles, and foundations of our American democracy, and the ability to participate in civic and democratic processes" (NCSS 2013, 31).

"Because government is a means for addressing common or public problems, the political system established by the U.S. Constitution is an important subject of study within civics. Civics requires other knowledge too; students should also learn about state and local governments; markets; courts and legal systems; civil society; other nations' systems and practices; international institutions; and the techniques available to citizens for preserving and changing a society" (NCSS 2013, 31).

Next, the Framework discusses why it is important to learn civic virtues:

"Civics is not limited to the study of politics and society; it also encompasses participation in classrooms and schools, neighborhoods, groups, and organizations. Not all participation is beneficial. This framework makes frequent reference to civic virtues (e.g., honesty, mutual respect, cooperation, seeing multiple perspectives) and principles that guide participation (e.g., equality, freedom, liberty, respect for individual rights) and to the norm of deliberation (discussing issues and making choices and judgments with information and evidence, civility and respect, and concern for fair procedures)" (NCSS 2013, 31).

And finally, the Framework describes how students practice engaged citizenship:

"In civics, students learn to contribute appropriately to public processes and discussions of real issues. Their contributions to public discussions may take many forms, ranging from personal testimony to abstract arguments. They will also learn civic practices such as voting, volunteering, jury service, and joining with others to improve society. Civics enables students not only to study how others participate but also to practice participating and taking informed action themselves" (NCSS 2013, 31).

Three Types of Civic Content Knowledge

The C3 Framework places the content for civics into three categories:

1. Civic and Political Institutions
2. Participation and Deliberation
3. Processes, Rules, and Laws

It specifies learning goals for grades 2, 5, 8, and 12, as shown in the following figures. Read vertically down each column to get a sense of what students should learn in each grade. Alternatively, read horizontally to get a sense of how the information builds and scaffolds as students advance from kindergarten to graduation.

Figure 2.1—*Suggested Pathway for Civic and Political Institutions*

By the End of Grade 2	By the End of Grade 5	By the End of Grade 8	By the End of Grade 12
Individually and with others, students...			
D2.Civ.1.K-2 Describe roles and responsibilities of people in authority.	**D2.Civ.1.3-5** Distinguish the responsibilities and powers of government officials at various levels and branches of government and in different times and places.	**D2.Civ.1.6-8** Distinguish the powers and responsibilities of citizens, political parties, interest groups, and the media in a variety of governmental and nongovernmental contexts.	**D2.Civ.1.9-12** Distinguish the powers and responsibilities of local, state, tribal, national, and international civic and political institutions.
D2.Civ.2.K-2 Explain how all people, not just official leaders, play important roles in a community.	**D2.Civ.2.3-5** Explain how a democracy relies on people's responsible participation, and draw implications for how individuals should participate.	**D2.Civ.2.6-8** Explain specific roles played by citizens (such as voters, jurors, taxpayers, members of the armed forces, petitioners, protesters, and office-holders).	**D2.Civ.2.9-12** Analyze the role of citizens in the U.S. political system, with attention to various theories of democracy, changes in Americans' participation over time, and alternative models from other countries, past and present.

By the End of Grade 2	By the End of Grade 5	By the End of Grade 8	By the End of Grade 12
Individually and with others, students...			
D2.Civ.3.K-2 Explain the need for and purposes of rules in various settings inside and outside of school.	**D2.Civ.3.3-5** Examine the origins and purposes of rules, laws, and key U.S. constitutional provisions.	**D2.Civ.3.6-8** Examine the origins, purposes, and impact of constitutions, laws, treaties, and international agreements.	**D2.Civ.3.9-12** Analyze the impact of constitutions, laws, treaties, and international agreements on the maintenance of national and international order.
D2.Civ.4.K-2 *Begins in grades 3–5*	**D2.Civ.4.3-5** Explain how groups of people make rules to create responsibilities and protect freedoms.	**D2.Civ.4.6-8** Explain the powers and limits of the three branches of government, public officials, and bureaucracies at different levels in the United States and in other countries.	**D2.Civ.4.9-12** Explain how the U.S. Constitution establishes a system of government that has powers, responsibilities, and limits that have changed over time and that are still contested.
D2.Civ.5.K-2 Explain what governments are and some of their functions.	**D2.Civ.5.3-5** Explain the origins, functions, and structure of different systems of government, including those created by the United States and state constitutions.	**D2.Civ.5.6-8** Explain the origins, functions, and structure of government with reference to the U.S. Constitution, state constitutions, and selected other systems of government.	**D2.Civ.5.9-12** Evaluate citizens' and institutions' effectiveness in addressing social and political problems at the local, state, tribal, national, and/or international level.

Figure 2.1—Suggested Pathway for Civic and Political Institutions (cont.)

By the End of Grade 2	By the End of Grade 5	By the End of Grade 8	By the End of Grade 12
Individually and with others, students...			
D2.Civ.6.K-2 Describe how communities work to accomplish common tasks, establish responsibilities, and fulfill roles of authority.	**D2.Civ.6.3-5** Describe ways in which people benefit from and are challenged by working together, including through government, workplaces, voluntary organizations, and families.	**D2.Civ.6.6-8** Describe the roles of political, civil, and economic organizations in shaping people's lives.	**D2.Civ.6.9-12** Critique relationships among governments, civil societies, and economic markets.

Figure 2.2—Suggested Pathway for Participation and Deliberation

By the End of Grade 2	By the End of Grade 5	By the End of Grade 8	By the End of Grade 12
Individually and with others, students...			
D2.Civ.7.K-2 Apply civic virtues when participating in school settings.	**D2.Civ.7.3-5** Apply civic virtues and democratic principles in school settings.	**D2.Civ.7.6-8** Apply civic virtues and democratic principles in school and community settings.	**D2.Civ.7.9-12** Apply civic virtues and democratic principles when working with others.
D2.Civ.8.K-2 Describe democratic principles such as equality, fairness, and respect for legitimate authority and rules.	**D2.Civ.8.3-5** Identify core civic virtues and democratic principles that guide government, society, and communities.	**D2.Civ.8.6-8** Analyze ideas and principles contained in the founding documents of the United States, and explain how they influence the social and political system.	**D2.Civ.8.9-12** Evaluate social and political systems in different contexts, times, and places, that promote civic virtues and enact democratic principles.
D2.Civ.9.K-2 Follow agreed-upon rules for discussions while responding attentively to others when addressing ideas and making decisions as a group.	**D2.Civ.9.3-5** Use deliberative processes when making decisions or reaching judgments as a group.	**D2.Civ.9.6-8** Compare deliberative processes used by a wide variety of groups in various settings.	**D2.Civ.9.9-12** Use appropriate deliberative processes in multiple settings.
D2.Civ.10.K-2 Compare their own point of view with others' perspectives.	**D2.Civ.10.3-5** Identify the beliefs, experiences, perspectives, and values that underlie their own and others' points of view about civic issues.	**D2.Civ.10.6-8** Explain the relevance of personal interests and perspectives, civic virtues, and democratic principles when people address issues and problems in government and civil society.	**D2.Civ.10.9-12** Analyze the impact and the appropriate roles of personal interests and perspectives on the application of civic virtues, democratic principles, constitutional rights, and human rights.

Figure 2.3—*Suggested Pathway for Processes, Rules, and Laws*

By the End of Grade 2	By the End of Grade 5	By the End of Grade 8	By the End of Grade 12
Individually and with others, students...			
D2.Civ.11.K-2 Explain how people can work together to make decisions in the classroom.	**D2.Civ.11.3-5** Compare procedures for making decisions in a variety of settings, including classroom, school, government, and/or society.	**D2.Civ.11.6-8** Differentiate among procedures for making decisions in the classroom, school, civil society, and local, state, and national government in terms of how civic purposes are intended.	**D2.Civ.11.9-12** Evaluate multiple procedures for making governmental decisions at the local, state, national, and international levels in terms of the civic purposes achieved.
D2.Civ.12.K-2 Identify and explain how rules function in public (classroom and school) settings.	**D2.Civ.12.3-5** Explain how rules and laws change society and how people change rules and laws.	**D2.Civ.12.6-8** Assess specific rules and laws (both actual and proposed) as means of addressing public problems.	**D2.Civ.12.9-12** Analyze how people use and challenge local, state, national, and international laws to address a variety of public issues.
D2.Civ.13.K-2 *Begins in grades 3–5*	**D2.Civ.13.3-5** Explain how policies are developed to address public problems.	**D2.Civ.13.6-8** Analyze the purposes, implementation, and consequences of public policies in multiple settings.	**D2.Civ.13.9-12** Evaluate public policies in terms of intended and unintended outcomes and related consequences.
D2.Civ.14.K-2 Describe how people have tried to improve their communities over time.	**D2.Civ.14.3-5** Illustrate historical and contemporary means of changing society.	**D2.Civ.14.6-8** Compare historical and contemporary means of changing societies and promoting the common good.	**D2.Civ.14.9-12** Analyze historical, contemporary, and emerging means of changing societies, promoting the common good, and protecting rights.

The EAD Report and Roadmap

The National Endowment for the Humanities and the U.S. Department of Education sponsored a multi-year effort with input from hundreds of experts and educators from a variety of ideological, philosophical, and demographic backgrounds. The group produced the *Educating for American Democracy (EAD) Report* and the accompanying *Roadmap to Educating for American Democracy* in March 2021.

Given how divided our country has been in recent years, the group was determined to lead by example:

> We made the project of arguing well together an overarching aspiration
> and, because of that focus, achieved more consensus than might have
> been anticipated at the outset. That purpose—inculcating skills and
> virtues for productive, civil disagreement—also takes pride of place within
> the Roadmap's guidance. (Educating for American Democracy 2021a, 8)

An Equity-Minded Approach to Civics and History Content

Historians and political scientists have made gains recently in the study of marginalized groups, social movements, and other areas that are not typically included in K–12 curricula. One of the aims of the EAD Report and Roadmap is to fix that. The report states that equitable civic education is not just a matter of spending money and distributing resources equitably. Rather, it is also about "intellectual and cultural resources," which includes the content and instruction in civic education. "Coming to a shared account of our past is essential to sharing equally the burdens of the work of the future," according to attorney and advocate Bryan Stevenson (2018). Academics and educators, he says, must achieve "an honest accounting of the past" to create "a more honest American identity" (Stevenson and Lewis 2018).

Because of the recent work of historians and political scientists, we now know more about the histories of women, Indigenous Americans, African Americans, immigrant communities, sexual minorities, and people with disabilities. It is important to include these stories in students' education. This means teaching about America, warts and all. For instance, how do we talk about great leaders and founders of our nation like George Washington and Thomas Jefferson while not concealing their history with slavery? Young people need to process America's contradictions while they are in school; otherwise, when they learn about this "hard history" later, they will find, as the EAD Report puts it, "their faith in our country existentially shaken" (2021a, 11). The EAD Roadmap takes all this into account.

An Inquiry-Based Approach

Like the C3 Framework, the EAD Roadmap takes an inquiry-based approach to civics and history. It is organized by major themes and questions, vertically spiraled across grade bands K–2, 3–5, 6–8, and 9–12 (Educating for American Democracy 2021c, para. 1). And like the C3 Framework, it is not a set of national standards but a "guide to the kinds of questions that should be asked and seriously engaged across the span of a K–12 education....The question of precisely how to help learners engage with these rich questions is left to state and local educational leaders and educators" (Educating for American Democracy 2021a, 12).

Civics and history are included together in the EAD materials. We will say more about how to teach them together in the next chapter but note that they are not two totally separate subjects, especially in K–5 education. In middle school and high school, students may learn about ancient civilizations mainly from a historical perspective, but even then, it's good to weave in civics concepts. If you are teaching about ancient Greece or Rome, for example, examine how certain modern fundamental democratic concepts, such as citizenship and voting, were present in their societies.

The Roadmap's Seven Themes

The EAD Roadmap is organized by seven major themes (Figure 2.4), each with questions and concepts. The document provides specific guidance for what to teach in grades K–8.

Figure 2.4—*EAD Roadmap Seven Content Themes*

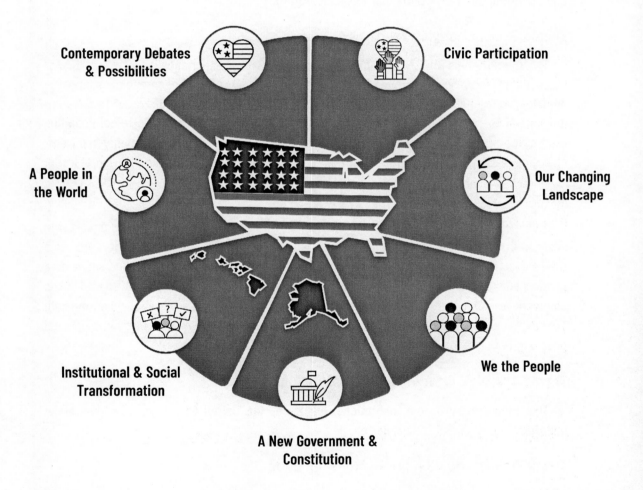

Theme 1: Civic Participation

This theme explores the relationship between self-government and civic participation, drawing on the discipline of history to explore how citizens' active engagement has mattered for American society and on the discipline of civics to explore the principles, values, habits, and skills that support productive engagement in a healthy, resilient constitutional democracy. This theme focuses attention on the overarching goal of engaging young people as civic participants and preparing them to assume that role successfully.

Theme 2: Our Changing Landscape

This theme begins with the recognition that American civic experience is tied to a particular place and explores how the United States developed its physical and geographical shape, the complex experiences of harm and benefit that American history has delivered to different portions of the American population, and the civics questions of how political communities form in the first place, become connected to specific places, and develop membership rules. This theme also takes up the question of our contemporary responsibility to the natural world.

Theme 3: We the People

This theme explores the idea of "We the People" as a political concept—beyond people who share a physical landscape to include people who share political ideals and institutions. This theme explores the history of how the contemporary American people have taken shape as a political body and builds civic understanding about how political institutions and shared ideals can work to connect a diverse population to shared processes of societal decision-making. This theme also explores the challenge of *E pluribus unum:* attempting to forge one political people out of diverse experiences.

Theme 4: A New Government & Constitution

This theme explores the institutional history of the United States and the theoretical underpinnings of constitutional design.

Theme 5: Institutional & Social Transformation

This theme explores how social arrangements and conflicts have combined with political institutions to shape American life from the earliest colonial period to the present, investigates which moments of change have most defined the country, and builds understanding of how American political institutions and society change.

Theme 6: A People in the World

This theme explores the United States and the American people in a global context, investigating key historical events in international affairs, and building understanding of the principles, values, and laws at stake in debates about America's role in the world.

Theme 7: Contemporary Debates & Possibilities

This theme explores the contemporary terrain of civic participation and civic agency, investigating how historical narratives shape current political arguments, how values and information shape policy arguments, and how the American people continue to renew or remake itself in pursuing fulfillment of the promise of constitutional democracy.

Questions and Concepts

The Roadmap provides driving questions and key concepts for each theme for grade bands from kindergarten to grade 12. Examples from Theme 1, Civic Participation, are included here:

Driving Questions, Grades K–2

History

★ How have I helped my class or family?

★ How do people describe who they are? How do I describe who I am?

★ How have people made our community better?

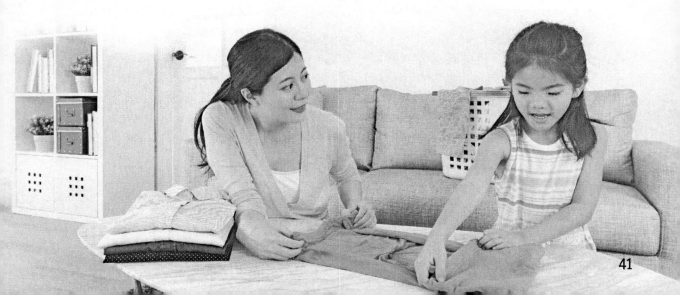

41

Civics

★ What does it mean to be a part of a group?

★ When/how do we speak up about something?

Driving Questions, Grades 3–5

History

★ Why and how do people take action in order to solve problems that affect them and others?

★ What kinds of challenges arise when people decide to take action to try to solve problems?

Civics

★ Why might we want to make changes at local, state, or national levels? How can we promote change in an effective way?

★ Why might you question decisions that are made for/in your community?

★ How can we work with others (even those who disagree with us) to help make change in society?

Driving Questions, Grades 6–8

History

★ When and where have leaders and changemakers emerged in American history? What has motivated them and prepared them for civic engagement?

★ What forms does civic participation take? Who has access to different forms of participation, and how has that access changed over time?

★ How has civic participation changed throughout American history? How has it stayed the same?

Civics

★ What matters to me, and why? How can I make what matters to me be about more than myself?

★ How do civil dialogue; investigation and analysis of issues; and civic action that is authentic, informed, and responsible strengthen our American constitutional democracy?

★ How can I take advantage of digital tools for civic participation safely and productively?

★ How can I engage as a member of my local, state, national, and global community? What opportunities or participation do I already have, and how can I engage with them?

★ What are "citizenship" and "civic agency" in general in America's constitutional democracy? How does voting relate to other forms of civic agency?

You can find the roadmap with complete list of driving questions and sample guiding questions, which are more detailed, at the Educating for American Democracy website: **www.educatingforamericandemocracy.org/the-roadmap**.

Tensions and Challenges

As noted in Chapter 1, the teaching of civics and history has the potential to be controversial. People in this country do not always agree about what children should learn. In their coverage of the EAD Report, *Education Week* reporters Stephen Sawchuk and Sarah Schwartz wrote about the effort to find that middle ground:

> Is America a land of freedom and opportunity, a shining civic example of government by and for the people? Or is it a system built on oppression and disenfranchisement that's forced marginalized peoples to fight for full participation? A set of K–12 history and civics guidelines...poses the question: What if it's both? (Sawchuk and Schwartz, 2021, para. 1)

The Design Challenges

The EAD Roadmap addresses the challenge of teaching civics in a polarized climate by providing five "Design Challenges." The challenges are derived from "design thinking," a process from the STEAM and business world, and they present the tensions and dilemmas teachers face.

A design challenge specifies a task and outlines the criteria for success. These are intended not for classroom teachers alone but also for people who write state standards, curricula, materials, and assessments. In fact, the EAD Roadmap makes a clear point about how everyone is in this together. The authors argue that the nation's entire community of educators *and* students should be included in the work necessary to find solutions: "Under the guidance of teachers well versed in the principles of the Roadmap, students, too, would become designers on the path to becoming knowledgeable and engaged citizens.... Educators and students alike will develop agency by facing contradictions that lack easy resolutions" (Educating for American Democracy 2021a, 17).

In other words, the process of wrestling with the design challenges builds student skills for healthy civic engagement. The design challenges provide valuable insight and are worth taking the time to read and reflect upon.

Design Challenge 1: Motivating Agency, Sustaining the Republic

- ★ How can we help students understand the full context for their role as citizens and civic participants without creating paralysis or a sense of the insignificance of their own agency in relation to the magnitude of our society, the globe, and shared challenges?

- ★ How can we help students become engaged citizens who also sustain civil disagreement, civic friendship, and thus American constitutional democracy?

- ★ How can we help students pursue civic action that is authentic, responsible, and informed?

Design Challenge 2: America's Plural Yet Shared Story

- ★ How can we integrate the perspectives of Americans from all different backgrounds when narrating a history of the United States and explicating the content of the philosophical foundations of American constitutional democracy?

★ How can we do so consistently across all of America's historical periods and conceptual content?

★ How can this more plural, and therefore more accurate, story of our history and foundations also be a common story, the shared inheritance of all Americans?

Design Challenge 3: Simultaneously Celebrating and Critiquing Compromise

★ How do we simultaneously teach the value and the danger of compromise for a free, diverse, and self-governing people?

★ How do we help students make sense of the paradox that Americans continuously disagree about the ideal shape of self-government but also agree to preserve shared institutions?

Design Challenge 4: Civic Honesty, Reflective Patriotism

★ How can we offer an account of U.S. constitutional democracy that is simultaneously honest about the past without falling into cynicism and appreciative of the founding without tipping into adulation?

Design Challenge 5: Balancing the Concrete and the Abstract

★ How can we support instructors in helping students move between concrete, narrative, and chronological learning and thematic and abstract or conceptual learning? (Educating for American Democracy 2021a)

About Reflective Patriotism

The EAD Report defines *reflective patriotism* as "appreciation of the ideals of our political order, candid reckoning with the country's failures to live up to those ideals, motivation to take responsibility for self-government, and deliberative skill to debate the challenges that face us in the present and future" (EAD 2021a, 12).

In January 2018, U.S. Senator Cory Booker said, "If this country hasn't broken your heart, you probably don't love her enough." That's a wonderful way of describing the kind of "reflective patriotism" we think should be the goal of civic education—you can love your country and also be aware of how it can be better. The word *patriot*, however, has recently become part of our partisan divide.

Some people may hesitate to call themselves patriots, seeing the moniker as an uncompromising "my country, right or wrong" stance. Some people may prefer to think of themselves as citizens who can love their community, if not the nation, until it earns it. People on this side of the debate may acknowledge the value of certain ideals upon which the nation was founded, but also point to shortfalls and hypocrisy. Still others see those who criticize the United States as unpatriotic. They find much to love about the country and point to progress that has been made to overcome the past and create a more just and inclusive society. Perhaps it is time to restore the word's reputation and broaden its definition and teach young people to be reflective patriots.

> Too often, we teach civics as activism. We encourage kids to protest. We encourage them to reform and change. We emphasize our nation's mistakes. All of that has its place. But it must lie on top of a solid foundation of understanding and respect for what we have.... America is unique and its maintenance requires a certain type of civics. We have to see civics as a user's manual for America.
>
> —Comment in "From Civic Education
> to a Civic Learning Ecosystem"
> (Vinnakota 2019, 29)

A Broader Conception of Patriotism

A common definition of *patriotism* is a feeling of devotion to a homeland, as well as an alliance with citizens who share the same sentiment. It is important to distinguish between patriotism and nationalism because they are sometimes used synonymously by people across the political spectrum. They are not synonyms. *Nationalism* is not only about loving your country but also gaining power for it, relative to other nations.

Nationalism was taken to extremes in Nazi Germany and fascist Italy during World War II. Historian Jill Lepore describes nationalism as, "less a love for your own country than a hatred of other countries and their people and a hatred of people in your country who don't belong to an ethnic, racial, or religious majority" (Lepore 2019, 23).

Steven B. Smith suggests rethinking what patriotism should mean in his 2021 book, *Reclaiming Patriotism in an Age of Extremes*. His main message is that patriotism can be critical, but it comes from a place of love and loyalty. Smith offers a message particularly relevant for those who teach civics: "American patriotism at its best does not rely on indoctrination but on teaching and supporting the virtues of civility, respect for law, respect for others, responsibility, honor, courage, loyalty, and leadership—all virtues worth having and keeping" (Smith 2021, 203).

From the *What* to the *How*

This chapter might be making you think the teaching of civics is kind of tricky in today's America. While it may not be as straightforward as teaching reading or mathematics, it is just as important. It can also be fun and very rewarding, which we will discuss in the next chapter.

Reflect and Apply

1. How will you know when your students have become (or are on their way to becoming) active citizens?

2. Do you tend to focus on names, dates, and events in your civics instruction? How can you focus more on conceptual ideas?

3. Think about how students in your school community might define *patriotism*. Is there a way to enhance their ideas about that notion in your classroom?

Chapter 3

Best Practices in Civic Education

In Chapter 1, we discussed why we need more and better civic education in this country. In Chapter 2, we talked about what civic education is and what it should include. In this chapter, we will look at how to teach civics in ways that engage your students and build civic understandings that will last a lifetime.

Recall that the three basic categories of what to teach in civics are:

★ Content knowledge

★ Skills and dispositions for citizenship

★ How to participate as a citizen in a democracy

This chapter covers each of these and provides examples of best practices.

Active Learning of Content, Skills, and Citizenship

Most people in America would agree that a certain basic set of facts and concepts is important for a good civic education. The debate is over *which* facts and concepts, as we discussed in Chapter 2. There is less debate, however, over *how* to teach facts and concepts, at least within education.

Students should not learn civics facts and concepts simply by memorizing them from a teacher's lecture, a textbook or worksheet, or their electronic or online equivalents. Memorizing is not even learning as educators and psychologists now know. Think about all the fact-based tests you took and how little information you retained the next year, month, or even week. For something to truly be "learned," it must stick with you—not word-for-word, but enough for you to be able to use it later (or at least recall that it's significant so you can look it up).

The rationale section of the C3 Framework states:

> The days are long past when it was sufficient to compel students to memorize other people's ideas and to hope that they would act on what they had memorized. If 20 years of National Assessment of Educational Progress report cards on youth civic, economic, geographical, and historical understanding mean anything, they repeatedly tell us that the success of that telling-and-compelling effort no longer works in the 21st century, if it ever did (Smith and Niemi 2001). (NCSS 2013, 89)

So, how should students gain knowledge of civics? How will they come to understand, for example, the three branches of government and why separation of powers is important? How will they learn how the president is elected or how laws are made? They do so by learning *actively*.

Active learning is just that: students are not sitting passively as the teacher pours knowledge into their empty heads. Instead, they are thinking about what they are learning and doing something with the information. They are connecting knowledge to what they already know and what they want to know. They are applying the knowledge to real situations and to their own lives.

According to the Center for Teaching Innovation at Cornell University, "Active learning methods ask students to fully participate in their learning by thinking, discussing, investigating, and creating. In active learning classrooms, students may be asked to practice skills, solve problems, struggle with complex questions, propose solutions, and explain ideas in their own words through writing and discussion" (n.d.). This approach can be traced to John Dewey, who advocated "learning by doing" early in the twentieth century. Active learning also connects the work of educators and theorists such as Maria Montessori, Jean Piaget, Lev Vygotsky, and Paolo Freire.

Just as active learning helps students gain content knowledge that they will retain, they can simultaneously gain the skills needed for democratic citizenship. It helps them think critically, evaluate information, use evidence in arguments, and discuss issues rationally with people they disagree with. They do this not by memorizing what concepts mean but by putting them into practice.

The same holds true for learning how to participate as a citizen. We wouldn't ask students simply to memorize the definition of *volunteerism* and a list of examples. To deeply learn about it, they would need to do research, consider their options, then actually volunteer somewhere. They don't learn best about elections through a lecture or a video about how they are held. They learn about elections by voting in the classroom or school or by playing a role in a real election in their community. They gain content knowledge as part of the process and in a way that internalizes it.

Combining It All

Active learning, therefore, teaches content, skills, and participatory citizenship at the same time. If students are working to inform their communities about local issues in an upcoming election, they would need to know the details about elections, such as when and where they are held. They would need to know who can vote, what a ballot is, and how the results are counted. They would need to decide what sources of information are trustworthy, think about and discuss the issues, and figure out what messages would work best for different voters. All the while, they are learning firsthand about the role citizens can play in creating a healthy democracy, even before they are old enough to vote.

Now let's look at how the two major civic education initiatives discussed in Chapter 2 incorporate active learning into their recommendations for teachers.

The C3 Framework and Active Learning

The C3 Framework recommends active learning in the form of an "Inquiry Arc" that focuses on the following four Dimensions of Inquiry:

1. Developing questions and planning inquiries

2. Applying disciplinary concepts and tools

3. Evaluating sources and using evidence

4. Communicating conclusions and taking informed action

The use of the term *arc* is significant; it means they are all connected. There is a first step, a pathway, and a destination. Here's what this looks like, with C3's examples:

Dimension 1: Developing Questions and Planning Inquiries

According to the C3 Framework, "the way to tie all of this content together" in civics is by using two types of questions: compelling and supporting. Compelling questions can come from the teacher or students. They focus on "enduring issues or concerns," not superficial questions. They are "both intriguing to students and intellectually honest," which means they're about something that truly is of concern to social scientists or historians. They "deal with curiosities about how things work; interpretations and applications of disciplinary concepts; and unresolved issues that require students to construct arguments in response" (NCSS 2013, 23).

Compelling questions are complex and open ended, with no agreed-upon right or wrong answer. For example, "Was the American Revolution revolutionary?" can be looked at from different points of view and debated. It appeals to students because it sounds contradictory and makes them reconsider impressions they might already have about the event.

An example from early elementary grades is, "Why are there rules?" That's inherently interesting to a child, who is subject to adult rules and likely wonders about them. There is also no simple "right answer" to the question. Some compelling questions can be answered by inquiry in one discipline. The question about rules, for example, is about civics. Others need to be explored from more than one discipline. Evaluating the American Revolution involves history, economics, geography, and civics.

Supporting questions can be generated by the teacher but often come from students, especially when students are older. These questions help a student answer a compelling question and are typically more about facts and concepts. As such, they are not quite as open-ended as compelling questions. In the American Revolution example, students might ask supporting questions, such as "What regulations were imposed by England on the colonists?" or "Why did some colonists oppose the Revolution?" or "Who were the people who led the Revolution?" In the elementary example about rules, students might ask, "What rules do families follow?" or "Who makes the rules?" or "What are some rules adults have to follow?"

Inquiry and Culturally and Linguistically Responsive Teaching

Inquiry-based lessons that take students into local communities support culturally and linguistically responsive teaching, which emphasizes making the curriculum more relevant to students and linking it to their languages, cultures, and communities (Ladson-Billings 1994). You will find the teaching of civics naturally provides many topics and issues that students can relate to and connect to their own cultural contexts.

Developmental Readiness for Inquiry

Younger students may have more difficulty asking compelling questions about civics. The C3 Framework makes it clear that teachers need to provide younger students with a lot of support for the process. They also give indicators that break down what students should be able to do in grades K–2, 3–5, 6–8, and 9–12. The concepts are laid out in Figure 3.1.

Figure 3.1—*Indicators for Compelling Questions*

By the End of Grade 2	By the End of Grade 5	By the End of Grade 8	By the End of Grade 12
Individually and with others, students...			
D1.1.K-2 Explain why the compelling question is important to the student.	**D1.1.3-5** Explain why compelling questions are important to others (e.g., peers, adults).	**D1.1.6-8** Explain how a question represents key ideas in the field.	**D1.1.9-12** Explain how a question reflects an enduring issue in the field.
D1.2.K-2 Identify disciplinary ideas associated with a compelling question.	**D1.2.3-5** Identify disciplinary concepts and ideas associated with a compelling question that are open to different interpretations.	**D1.2.6-8** Explain points of agreement experts have about interpretations and applications of disciplinary concepts and ideas associated with a compelling question.	**D1.2.9-12** Explain points of agreement and disagreement experts have about interpretations and applications of disciplinary concepts and ideas associated with a compelling question.

Determining Helpful Sources

Dimension 1 also asks students to decide where to find answers to their questions. Again, teachers need to support this process. Young students need to know the kinds of sources to use and where to find information. Older students need to consider differing opinions and alternate points of view on the topic. Sources of information and evidence can come in many forms. It could be the teacher's own knowledge; textbooks, news reports, and other secondary sources; or information can be gathered from primary sources, such as historical and contemporary documents, government websites, the U.S. Constitution and Declaration of Independence, and court rulings.

Dimension 2: Applying Disciplinary Concepts and Tools

This is the phase of the Inquiry Arc when students learn to use the basics of civics as a lens to apply to their investigation. In contrast to traditional instruction that includes a lot of memorization, however, students understand that they are learning the material for a larger purpose. They are preparing to answer the compelling question.

Typical state curricular content standards specify exactly what students should learn in each grade level. The C3 Framework focuses more on bigger ideas, concepts, and skills within a grade band. In Chapter 2, we discussed the three categories for the content of civics: civic and political institutions; participation and deliberation; and processes, rules, and laws.

Dimension 3: Evaluating Sources and Using Evidence

As students build their knowledge of disciplinary concepts and tools and find sources of information, they need to evaluate the quality of their sources. "Not all sources are equal in value," the C3 Framework points out, and many may not provide good evidence for a claim.

As students move to the fourth phase of the Inquiry Arc, they will need to back up their explanations and arguments with evidence. This is a key skill for democratic citizenship.

Dimension 4: Communicating Conclusions and Taking Informed Action

This is where the active learning in the Inquiry Arc ultimately leads. After asking questions, learning about the disciplines, and evaluating evidence, students *do* something. They either communicate their answers in public venues, meaning with someone other than their teacher, or they combine that with taking action. Students should collaborate with others in this phase.

Communicating and Critiquing Conclusions

Students can communicate their answers to the compelling questions with evidence in a variety of ways:

★ Essays in a particular genre, such as persuasive or informational writing, which could be a letter to a state or national legislator or an opinion piece to a local newspaper

★ A speech delivered to an audience, or an opinion statement read on a local radio station

★ Authentic written products, such as a report for a particular purpose and audience, a mock "policy brief" for a government official, or a ruling by a judge in a role-played mock trial

★ Multimedia presentations, podcasts, videos (e.g., public service announcements shown to other students or parents, uploaded to a website, or shown on local TV)

For some of the formats described above, you may need students to complete more than one task to fully demonstrate both their understandings of the material and their ability to construct arguments. A single, substantial essay may contain enough for assessment purposes. But a multimedia presentation or an authentic written product may not provide enough evidence of the knowledge and conceptual understanding gained, or it may simply not be appropriate to include all that detail in an authentic product.

Consider the example of a video public service announcement produced by a team of students. The script is going to contain a lot fewer words than an essay or written report. It's a distillation of students' understandings, not a complete package. To assess adequately what students have learned, you might also ask students to submit written explanations of the choices they made. This is even more necessary when the product is created by a team of students; you can ask each student to write an explanation individually.

For younger students who may not be able to express themselves in writing yet, you'll need to do what you always do to assess their understanding: observe what they do and talk with them. The C3 Framework breaks this down into grade-level bands as shown in Figure 3.2.

Figure 3.2—Assessing Understanding

By the End of Grade 2	By the End of Grade 5	By the End of Grade 8	By the End of Grade 12
Individually and with others, students...			
D4.1.K-2 Construct an argument with reasons.	**D4.1.3-5** Construct arguments using claims and evidence from multiple sources.	**D4.1.6-8** Construct arguments using claims and evidence from multiple sources, while acknowledging the strengths and limitations of the arguments.	**D4.1.9-12** Construct arguments using precise and knowledgeable claims, with evidence from multiple sources, while acknowledging counterclaims and evidentiary weaknesses.
D4.2.K-2 Construct explanations using correct sequence and relevant information.	**D4.2.3-5** Construct explanations using reasoning, correct sequence, examples, and details with relevant information and data.	**D4.2.6-8** Construct explanations using reasoning, correct sequence, examples, and details with relevant information and data, while acknowledging the strengths and weaknesses of the explanations.	**D4.2.9-12** Construct explanations using sound reasoning, correct sequence (linear or non-linear), examples, and details with significant and pertinent information and data, while acknowledging the strengths and weaknesses of the explanation given its purpose.

The Need for Critique

In addition to communicating their own conclusions, students should also have opportunities to critique others' ideas. This helps to deepen their understandings of concepts and tools in civics and also helps them build skills and attitudes that will help in their further education, on the job, and as citizens in a democracy. Respectfully disagreeing with other citizens—or knowing how to critique with arguments and evidence—is absolutely vital, so students should learn how to do it from an early age.

There are many places to find critique protocols for students. One of the most comprehensive collections is from the National School Reform Faculty (**www.nsrfharmony.org**).

Making a Real-World Impact

The C3 Framework points out that when students learn civics by actually doing something in the real world, it not only supports college and career readiness but also the third goal of the Framework: readiness for civic life. Taking informed action is where it all comes together: civic knowledge, skills, attitudes, and dispositions.

Making a real-world impact can take many forms, both in school (since that's part of a student's real world) and outside it. Students have many options to take action by communicating their conclusions to a public audience, including:

★ Present to external stakeholders about a local issue they have researched. Community members could visit the classroom, students could present to an online audience, or students could visit members of the community.

★ Plan and carry out a social media campaign to inform and influence others about an issue.

★ Contribute to the work of an organization that helps communities; promotes democracy; or addresses community, state, national or global issues.

★ Take action in other forms of civic engagement, such as making decisions within the classroom, working to affect school or district policies, or starting or leading organizations in the school.

Find more examples of lessons and projects in which students communicate their conclusions publicly and take informed action in Chapter 5.

The EAD Pedagogy Companion and Active Learning

Like the C3 Framework, the *Educating for American Democracy (EAD) Pedagogy Companion* emphasizes inquiry and active citizenship. In addition to the design challenges and content themes (discussed in Chapter 2), the companion adds six core pedagogical principles (Figure 3.3). Each comes with helpful, practical "moves" for teachers, students, and school and community leaders.

Figure 3.3—The EAD Teacher

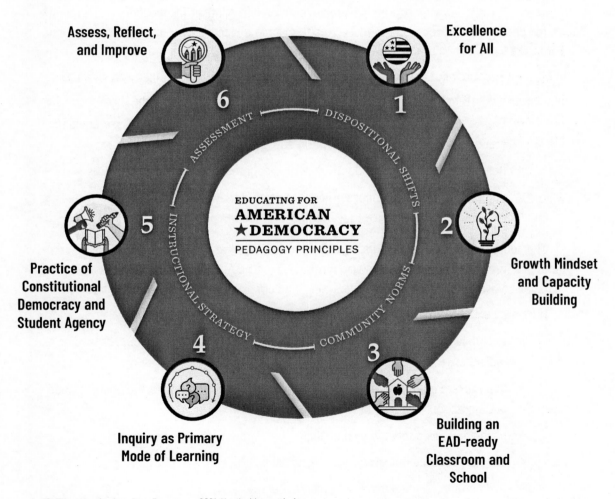

EDUCATING FOR
AMERICAN ★ DEMOCRACY
PEDAGOGY PRINCIPLES

1 — Excellence for All — DISPOSITIONAL SHIFTS

2 — Growth Mindset and Capacity Building — COMMUNITY NORMS

3 — Building an EAD-ready Classroom and School

4 — Inquiry as Primary Mode of Learning — INSTRUCTIONAL STRATEGY

5 — Practice of Constitutional Democracy and Student Agency

6 — Assess, Reflect, and Improve — ASSESSMENT

The first pedagogical principle, "Excellence for All," has to do with a teacher's mindset regarding civics and history. This principle asks teachers to:

★ Commit to learn about and teach full and multifaceted historical and civic narratives.

★ Appreciate student diversity and assume all students' capacity for learning complex and rigorous content.

★ Focus on inclusion and equity in both content and approach.

The next two pedagogical principles focus on a growth mindset for teachers and students and on creating a classroom and school culture that supports active learning and civil discourse. These are sample "teacher moves" for the latter:

★ Intentionally seek to learn more about students and their families and strive to build relationships with and among students.

★ Create opportunities through a variety of discussion structures and protocols for students to understand diverse perspectives.

★ Help students engage productively with disagreements and solve conflicts.

★ Support students to process emotionally difficult events using different modes of expression, including dialogue, writing, and creating art.

The fourth principle includes using various teaching strategies to support inquiry, from direct instruction (in its more complex forms, not just lectures). This includes discussions, debates, investigations, project-based learning, and simulations of democratic processes.

Here are some teacher moves to support this principle:

★ Design lessons that uncover the complexity of an event, social group, or leading individual.

★ Incorporate opportunities to analyze diverse forms of evidence, including images and texts.

★ Introduce new concepts by building on background knowledge.

★ Engage students in historical-thinking skills.

★ Build student engagement with media literacy.

The fifth principle is about taking action: Practice of Constitutional Democracy and Student Agency. The teacher moves include the following:

★ Provide students the opportunity to practice democratic skills in the classroom.

★ Facilitate opportunities for students to interact with community leaders, initiatives, and issues.

★ Facilitate opportunities for students to take informed action in their communities.

★ Design lessons to support student research skills, including data collection, conducting interviews, and reporting findings.

The sixth principle is about assessment, reflection, and continuous improvement (Educating for American Democracy 2021b). The entire guide is a thoughtful, comprehensive document, worth reading from start to finish.

Teaching Civil Discourse

As we said earlier, civic education in a democracy must include learning how to talk with one another. It must teach students how to engage in civil discourse. In President Joe Biden's Inaugural Address on January 20, 2021, he said, "We must end this uncivil war that pits red against blue, rural versus urban, conservative versus liberal." He echoed a sentiment from now-retired Senator Orrin Hatch (2017), who said:

> "Civility is the indispensable political norm. It is the public virtue that has greased the wheels of our democracy since its inception. Although nowhere mandated in our Constitution, civility is no less essential to the proper functioning of our government than any amendment, court ruling or act of Congress. Without it, little separates us from the cruelty and chaos of rule by force."

Civil discourse is not simply about being "polite." That may be part of it, but overemphasizing politeness can sometimes prevent people from saying what must be said. According to the Charles Koch Institute (2018):

> "Politeness does not fully encompass what civility is.... Civil discourse is not polite conversation that simply clutches its pearls in horror at crassness. Civil discourse is conversation with a serious purpose. It is

conversation that looks to find shared opportunity, not conflict.
It is conversation that looks to remove barriers, not build new
ones. It is a conversation that instead of becoming paralyzed by our
disagreements, uses them to propel creative solutions and alternatives."

This may sound like a tall order. After all, young people today see incivility everywhere, from social media and cable TV news to pop culture and sporting events. But as a teacher of civics, you can help provide students with a foundation in civil discourse that will carry them into their lives as citizens.

Best Practices for Teaching Civil Discourse

Much has been written recently about how to teach civil discourse. Most of it is focused on middle and high school, but it can be applied to elementary students as well. The following material is drawn from two organizations: Facing History and Ourselves (**facinghistory.org**) and Learning for Justice (**learningforjustice.org**) (formerly Teaching Tolerance), whose websites contain more details and resources.

1. **Examine your own beliefs, politics, and emotions so you can keep learning goals objective when it comes to civics-related issues.** Reflect on your own context. What perspectives do you have, and how might this differ from how others view the world? What topics might you find difficult to bring up in the classroom, and why?

2. **Create a classroom community, and build trust.** Build relationships by getting to know your students and helping them learn about one another by sharing aspects of their identities and lived experiences. Form emotional bonds through team-builders and other shared, enjoyable experiences.

3. **Co-create norms for discourse with students.** These are sometimes called community agreements, ground rules, or even a "contract." Ask students to suggest ideas, such as "It's okay to disagree respectfully" or "No put-downs" or "Listen to understand." Narrow the list down to four to six items, write them on a poster, and put them on the wall. Be sure to revisit the norms before every discussion and check with students periodically to see if the list needs revision. Be aware that students' cultural backgrounds may have different norms around speaking in public or how civics-related issues are discussed—or are not

discussed—in the home.

4. **Set goals for a discussion.** Don't just make the discourse a formless free-for-all. Possible goals could be to reach agreement on an action or to outline the key points of both sides of an issue.

5. **Ask students to prepare before a whole-group discussion.** Ask students to prepare by doing some reading, making notes, and outlining their ideas—it could be anywhere from 10 minutes beforehand to a day or two in advance. Also, be sure to allow time for students to reflect and then share with partners or in small groups to prime the pump for whole-group discourse.

6. **Teach students how to make an argument.** Discuss how an opinion is different from an argument. Teach the three "ARE" parts of an argument—assertion, reasoning, and evidence—with lots of examples. Discuss what makes evidence solid and reliable.

7. **Establish routines for discussions.** Help students get familiar with how things are done every time. One possible routine may be to have 10 minutes of prep time, 2 minutes for norm review, 20 minutes for discussion, and 5 minutes for reflection and debriefing.

Unsung Heroes of Civic Education

Lots of civic learning takes place outside of civics classes . . . elementary school teachers regularly teach and model behaviors and attitudes that are essential to helping young people develop into productive citizens: the ability to share, cooperate, take other people's perspectives into account, negotiate, and so on. They're doing essential work but with little recognition or support.

—Raj Vinnakota, President, Institute for Citizens & Scholars (2019)

How Civic Education Supports Social-Emotional Learning (SEL)

When you teach civics in the ways we discuss in this book, you are also building students' social-emotional competency. The Collaborative for Academic, Social, and Emotional Learning (CASEL) developed a framework for SEL with five core competencies:

1. **Self-Awareness**
   The abilities to understand one's own emotions, thoughts, and values and how they influence behavior across contexts

2. **Self-Management**
   The abilities to manage one's emotions, thoughts, and behaviors effectively in different situations and to achieve goals and aspirations

3. **Responsible Decision-Making**
   The abilities to make caring and constructive choices about personal behavior and social interactions across diverse situations

4. **Relationship Skills**
   The abilities to establish and maintain healthy and supportive relationships and to effectively navigate settings with diverse individuals and groups

5. **Social Awareness**
   The abilities to understand the perspectives of and empathize with others, including those from diverse backgrounds, cultures, and contexts

These competencies come into play often in civic education. Many of the topics and issues students learn about in civics will cause students to reflect on their own emotions, thoughts, and values. Students will need self-management and relationship skills, plus decision-making and social awareness, when they engage with others in civic discourse and when they participate in activities and projects whose goal is to make a real-world impact (CASEL, n.d.).

How to Approach Controversial Issues

Many teachers in this time of highly charged, polarized politics shy away from bringing controversial issues into their classrooms. They fear that it could generate conflict among students, and parents might be upset. They might be discouraged by administrators who would rather not hear from angry parents or find their school in a media spotlight. And it's challenging to get the teaching of controversial issues right. Nevertheless, we encourage you to bring these difficult topics into your classroom.

Benefits of Including Controversial Issues

Diana Hess and Paula McAvoy (2014) write of the need to teach controversial issues in the classroom, noting that it is necessary to teach students to "deliberate about their differences." Furthermore, civic education without controversial issues is "like a symphony without sound," says Hess. She argues that including controversial issues in the curriculum "can communicate by example the essence of what makes communities democratic while simultaneously building the skills and dispositions that young people will need to live in and improve such communities."

Research shows that giving students the opportunity to discuss current issues and events in the classroom increases their interest in civic life and politics and leads to improved critical thinking and communication skills (Gould et al. 2011). Further, iCivics (2020) notes that including controversial issues in civic education helps students develop:

- ★ **Skills for Life:** thinking critically, analyzing information, problem-solving, negotiating
- ★ **Skills for the Modern World:** communicating clearly, listening actively, engaging in civil discourse, respecting differences
- ★ **Skills for Active Citizenship:** compromising, decision-making, moral/ethical reasoning, applying abstract ideas

From "Safe" Classrooms to "Brave" Classrooms

Educators who want to foster inclusive and equitable schools typically talk about making them "safe" places. Classroom norms might reflect this, such as giving respect to others, showing empathy, maintaining confidentiality, assuming positive intent, and being sensitive to others' emotions.

In civic education, however, we need to move beyond safety to bravery. Students might think safety means they must always be "polite" and never disagree, never ask difficult questions, or never make someone else uncomfortable. That only goes so far when discussing our nation's history and politics. And students might feel differently about certain norms for safety; for example, those from marginalized groups might not be able to "assume positive intent" given the history of oppression in the United States (Arao and Clemens 2013).

According to the Anti-Defamation League (n.d.), "A brave space is one in which we accept that we will feel uncomfortable and maybe even defensive...one in which we take risks, doing so with care and compassion." To make your classroom a "brave space," the ADL suggests asking students to define *brave* and share their thoughts about why it's sometimes important. Then, cogenerate a list of guidelines for bravery in the classroom (which you could post on the wall as a reminder), such as:

- ★ Be open to different and multiple viewpoints and perspectives, especially those that differ from yours.
- ★ If people share experiences and feelings that are different or unfamiliar to you, show respect by taking them seriously, and understand the impact of your response.
- ★ Make space by sharing speaking time; try to speak after others who have not spoken.
- ★ Listen actively, even and especially when people say things that are difficult to hear.
- ★ View the candor of others as a gift.
- ★ Work hard not to be defensive if people challenge what you say or the impact of your words.

Choosing Which Controversial Issues to Include in Civics

It may be tempting to always choose a current event when discussing controversial issues. Students may also be eager to discuss something they've been hearing about in the news or in family conversations. At times, a current event will be the right choice, but at others it might not be. There are other ways to choose controversial issues:

1. **Be sure the issue can be leveraged to teach civics content and concepts.** A dispute between the president and Congress over a government spending bill can be used to teach the concept of separation of powers. Or a local issue about how a city handled a protest could help teach about free speech and individual rights.

2. **Consider the age of your students.** You know your students and community best, so it's your call as to when and how to introduce controversial issues. It might be appropriate for middle and high schoolers to discuss national immigration policy, for example, but that may not be appropriate for young students. Primary-age children could still practice the same skills for civil discourse with a more age-appropriate topic. To them, an issue such as "Are the new rules for the lunchroom fair?" would be highly engaging.

3. **Choose the issues carefully.** Many controversial issues can be personal for students. They may involve their identities and could potentially trigger a range of emotions. Watch out for issues that could pit one group of students against another, especially if one is composed of students from a marginalized group. These may still be appropriate to discuss, but be careful to follow norms and frame the issues appropriately.

4. **Start with issues that are not "hot button" issues.** When students are new to the process and still learning the norms for discussing controversial issues, the Learning for Justice project suggests giving them "training wheels." Instead of starting with a current event about a racial issue, for example, start small with something such as whether the city should put a park or an apartment building on some vacant land.

Teaching Strategies for Controversial Issues

Educator Kate Shuster (n.d.) offers this helpful advice for how to teach a controversial issue:

★ **Break the issue into parts:** Most civic-related issues are complex, so unpack them for students. Think about what knowledge and concepts they will need in order to understand and discuss it.

★ **Build a list of relevant vocabulary words associated with the issue:** Keep a list from readings and research, and teach the words just as you would for any other instructional topic.

★ **Select readings that will be accessible and also challenging:** You might need to do some digging to find articles or other sources of information—from different points of view on the issue—that your students can read and comprehend. See the differentiated reading level versions of articles on various topics at **Newsela.com**.

★ **Require a culminating activity:** After reading about and discussing a current event or controversial issue, don't leave them hanging. Have students do something to synthesize what they learned. They could write persuasive or informative essays or letters to their legislative representatives. Engage them in roundtable discussions, or have them make presentations to outside organizations. If the examination of an issue connects directly to their work on a project, have students incorporate what they have learned into their plans for the project.

★ **Debrief:** Ask students to reflect on what they have learned, how well they followed norms for discussions, or how easy it was to trace the development of their thinking about a topic. This could be the culminating activity or it could be a separate step.

Additional Tips

★ Set norms/community agreements about how controversial issues will be handled in your classroom.

★ To scaffold discussion skills and reinforce norms such as "disagree respectfully," provide students with sentence stems, such as "I see what you're saying, but I have another idea" or "Another way to look at it is...."

★ Avoid spontaneous discussions. Plan ahead to teach controversial issues, and manage discussions to keep them focused on targeted learning goals.

★ Be careful about injecting your own political views into the classroom. Students (and their parents) may object if it feels like you're attempting to influence them in a partisan way. This is a judgment call; there may be a pedagogical purpose for revealing or withholding your views.

Check out these resources for more information on teaching controversial issues and current events:

- ★ "Your Roadmap for Teaching Controversial Issues" (iCivics) **www.icivics.org/professional-development/your-roadmap-teaching-controversial-issues**

- ★ *Civil Discourse in the Classroom: Teaching Controversy* (Learning for Justice) **www.learningforjustice.org/magazine/publications/civil-discourse-in-the-classroom/chapter-4-teaching-controversy**

- ★ *Controversy in the Classroom: The Democratic Power of Discussion* by Diana E. Hess (2009)

- ★ *The Political Classroom: Evidence and Ethics in Democratic Education* by Diana E. Hess and Paula McAvoy (2014)

Reconsidering Debates: Try the "Structured Academic Controversy" Format Instead

Debates have been a long-time feature of civic education. They teach students how to construct arguments and support those arguments with valid evidence. They teach students how to speak and listen to others. Traditional debates, however, also have drawbacks that are leading civics and history educators to rethink them and find alternatives.

According to **TeachingHistory.org**, debates can cause students to think every issue comes neatly packaged in a pro/con format and that the goal is to win, as opposed to have a discussion and truly listen. The organization suggests "shifting the goal from winning classroom discussions to understanding alternative positions and formulating historical syntheses" using a format called "Structured Academic Controversy."

In this approach, students learn to listen in new ways and come to understand the complexity of controversial ideas. The emphasis is on deliberation, hearing varied perspectives, and the possibility of changing your own mind, as opposed to winning a debate. This aligns with standards for speaking and listening that emphasize acknowledging new information expressed by others and, when warranted, modifying one's own views.

For information on how to conduct a Structured Academic Controversy, including examples and interesting topics, visit **TeachingHistory.org**.

Information Literacy

Former teacher and principal Dale Chu (2021) recently wrote about what he believes is needed to cure the divisions in this country: "Perhaps what's really needed is a recommitment to the values of the Enlightenment: reason, facts, and science." He goes on to argue that we need a "curriculum that trains students to think critically and instills a respect, even a reverence, for knowledge and evidence," and notes that "the Founding Fathers prized reason and wisdom, regarding a well-educated citizenry as requisite to our survival as a free people" (Chu 2021).

This underscores one of your key roles as a civics educator: teaching students how to handle the information they will be inundated with every day as a citizen in this country. Chu is also thinking about math and science education, but there are many ways you can bring critical thinking and "reverence for knowledge and evidence" into civics.

Information literacy has gone by many different names in the past, including media literacy, civic literacy, and digital literacy. But the basic idea is the same: teaching students how to find the truth in a sea of misinformation and manipulation. You can start teaching information literacy with even young children, by calling it "knowing what's true and what's a lie." With older students, you could call it "identifying fake information and understanding real news and information you can trust."

Even for adults, navigating today's information landscape requires a great deal of skill. You can help prepare young people for citizenship in a technology-fueled, information-cluttered democracy. Teach information literacy with stand-alone lessons, activities, and projects and by infusing it into your instruction whenever possible and appropriate.

There are many resources to help you teach information literacy:

Learning for Justice
learningforjustice.org
This organization offers a framework describing seven areas in which students need support, with detailed accompanying lessons for grades K–2, 3–5, 6–8, and 9–12. Go to
www.learningforjustice.org/frameworks/digital-literacy. The article "Learning the Landscape of Digital Literacy" on this website is also very helpful.

iCivics
iCivics.org

There are many information literacy resources on this website, including several for middle and high school teachers:

★ The video game "NewsFeed Defenders" lets students fight hidden ads, search for viral deception, and hunt for false reporting.

★ Lesson 1: Journalism helps students learn what separates journalism from other kinds of information and to recognize reliable reporting.

★ Lesson 2: Misinformation teaches students to examine news stories for evidence of transparency and verification that will help them distinguish legitimate news from unreliable information.

Stanford History Education Group
sheg.stanford.edu

This website has a "Civic Online Reasoning" curriculum for middle and high school, with workshops for teachers and free lessons, videos, and assessments. Its goal is to help students become more skilled evaluators of online content by using a process derived from fact-checkers, based on three questions: Who's behind the information?; What's the evidence?; and What do other sources say?

"Website Research: CRAAP Test"
libguides.cmich.edu/web_research/craap

This guide to website research is for college students and adults, but you could easily adapt it for younger students. It provides five criteria: Currency, Relevance, Authority, Accuracy, and Purpose (CRAAP), with questions to ask and typical issues in evaluating online sources of information.

"5 Essential Steps to Teach Information Literacy in Middle School"
www.aeseducation.com/blog/5-essential-steps-to-teach-information-literacy-in-middle-school

This article has excellent practical advice for secondary teachers, with an emphasis on how to determine whether information is trustworthy.

Civic Education beyond the Classroom

From sports to clubs, there are many places students can get an education in civics in addition to the classroom. Schools can also do things to promote democratic values and principles, build leadership skills, and encourage active citizenship through service learning, involving students in school governance, and extracurricular activities.

Service Learning

Service learning has many benefits. It's motivating for young people. It helps them connect knowledge of civics and democratic values with powerful real-world experiences. When students do a project that serves others, volunteer with a community organization, or join a larger cause, research shows it's a strong predictor of civic engagement later in life. What's more, service learning has been shown to especially benefit students in lower-income communities.

According to the National Youth Leadership Council (2008), high-quality service learning should:

1. have sufficient duration and intensity to address community needs and meet specified outcomes;

2. be used intentionally as an instructional strategy to meet learning goals and/or content standards;

3. incorporate multiple challenging reflection activities that are ongoing and that prompt deep thinking and analysis about oneself and one's relationship to society;

4. actively engage participants in meaningful and personally relevant service activities;

5. promote understanding of diversity and mutual respect among all participants;

6. be collaborative and mutually beneficial and address community needs;

7. engage participants in an ongoing process to assess the quality of implementation and progress toward meeting specified goals and use results for improvement and sustainability;

8. provide youth with a strong voice in planning, implementing, and evaluating service-learning experiences with guidance from adults.

You can find many resources online about service learning, including:

National Youth Leadership Council
www.nylc.org/page/WhatisService-Learning

Curriculum Design Toolkit: Service Learning
www.illinoiscivics.org/curriculum-design/service-learning

School Governance

Involving students in governing the school could range from the traditional student council that makes decisions about a limited set of activities to a more fully "democratic" system where students have some degree of real power in the school. According to a report on the civic mission of schools, "A long tradition of research suggests that giving students more opportunities to participate in the management of their own classrooms and schools builds their civic skills and attitudes" (Gould et al. 2011, 33). Regarding the traditional models of student involvement, the report notes:

> "Student councils should be far more than the social planners of the school; they should instead stimulate and engage large numbers of students in school and community service activities and provide a forum for student voice on questions that impact the students themselves" (Gould et al. 2011).

Research by the National Association of Student Councils shows that student participation in school governance should meet specific criteria:

1. Activities must be structured.

2. Students must make a substantial time commitment to activities.

3. Activities must engage student interest.

4. Students' decisions must have real effects (Gould et al. 2011).

Extracurricular Activities

Many different kinds of extracurricular activities can help students build skills and dispositions for democratic citizenship. They include sports, clubs, journalism, performing arts, as well as more explicitly civic activities, such as model Congress, mock trial, speech and debate, and model United Nations.

Research has shown that extracurricular activities "provide opportunities to acquire and practice skills that may be useful in a wide variety of settings [to] help students to develop a sense of agency as a member of one's community; to belong to a socially recognized and valued group, to develop support networks of peers and adults that can help in both present and future; and to experience and deal with challenges" (Eccles et al. 2003).

"Extracurricular activities are a vital part of well-rounded civic learning," according to Jonathan Gould et al. (2011). "Given that the goal of civic learning on the whole is to prepare students for knowledgeable, engaged citizenship, extracurricular activities can serve as a vital bridge between classroom learning and the world at large. Once students have the essential knowledge that comes from classroom instruction, extracurricular activities can show them how their newly acquired knowledge is relevant in broader contexts" (Gould et al. 2011).

Teacher Jennifer Levin-Goldberg (2009) gives advice for making extracurricular activities effective. She outlines four key components:

1. **Alignment to political knowledge or skills:** Students must learn more than the background knowledge to their concern; they must also acquire the skills necessary to behaviorally solve and assist their cause.

2. **Accessibility:** Some students may have family duties, transportation issues, or other challenges that make it difficult to participate. Try to accommodate them by adjusting meeting times and helping them figure out how to meet challenges.

3. **Student interest:** Don't force students to participate in activities that don't engage them. Find out what students' interests are, and find activities that are a good fit.

4. **Serving the greater good:** Since the goal is to engender civic engagement, activities must be directed at benefitting others, not just the individual.

Onward!

Hopefully, you're feeling even more confident and proud to teach civics. We've discussed the urgent need for civic education in our country, explored some of the challenges, and explained some current thinking and our view of what should be taught and how. In the next chapter, we'll take a look at how to teach literacy in civics and then move on to share some teaching resources that will help you put your students on the path to informed, committed, and active democratic citizenship.

Reflect and Apply

1. How frequently do you implement active learning for civics instruction? What is one active-learning strategy you would like to implement?

2. Think about how your students might respond to a discussion about a controversial issue. How could you best introduce it so that it could be discussed in a productive manner?

3. What opportunities are there for service learning in your community? Whom might you be able to contact to engage your students in learning outside the classroom?

Chapter 4

Integrating Literacy in Civic Education

Most educators know that it is important to integrate literacy across the content areas. Literacy, after all, is about communication of ideas and information. This is done through reading and writing as well as listening and speaking. This can be accomplished with civic education in two very natural ways: integrating literacy into civic education and integrating civic education into reading and language arts programs. Teaching content-area literacy in civics is about teaching literacy skills through the subject of civics or using civics topics within a reading and language arts program.

What Is Content-Area Literacy?

Content-area literacy is defined as "the ability to use reading and writing to learn a subject matter in a particular discipline" and "emphasizes a set of study skills that can be used across content-areas" (Chauvin and Theodore 2015, 2). Teachers model for students how to think about texts, how to preview vocabulary, how to evaluate and interpret what is read, and how to communicate thoughts and ideas verbally and through writing. Content-rich ELA instruction in the early grades can help develop and influence linguistic comprehension, leading to a better overall understanding of a topic (Cabell and Hwang 2020).

Seibert et al. (2016) discuss the need for reform in content-area instruction, claiming that students need to be active participants in a discipline, rather than simply gaining knowledge about it. They say, "Although subject matter knowledge—terms, facts, concepts, and skills—is still valued, reformers often envision knowledge being produced through or acquired during engagement in disciplinary practices...." (26). Likewise, they emphasize the importance of student participation in the literacies that are necessary for making sense of a discipline. They recommend changing the focus from learning literacies (i.e., predicting, summarizing) to participating in them.

English Language Arts Standards and Civics

The College and Career Readiness Standards—and most state standards—support an inquiry-based, active-learning approach to civic education. The connections are clear in the reading standards, the writing standards, and in the relatively new standards for speaking and listening, which also support active citizenship. College and Career Readiness Standards address media literacy as well, another key to civic education.

The C3 Framework emphasizes the connection and alignment with the College and Career Readiness Standards. This is demonstrated by terms used in the standards, such as *argument* and *explanation; claim* and *counterclaim; information* and *evidence;* and *point of view* and *opinion.*

Figure 4.1—C3 Framework Dimension 1: Developing Questions and Planning Inquiries

College and Career Readiness ELA Standard	Civics Connection
Ask and answer questions to demonstrate understanding of a text; draw inferences; cite specific textual evidence when writing or speaking.	Students' ability to ask questions is key to the inquiry process. They gather information through reading and research. Some information from civics-related text will be factual, some will be based on inference.
Conduct... research projects based on focused questions, demonstrating understanding of the subject under investigation.	Students pose and/or address "compelling questions" to focus their inquiry, plus more specific "supporting questions."
Prepare for and participate effectively in a range of conversations and collaborations with diverse partners, building on others' ideas and expressing their own clearly and persuasively.	Much of civic education is collaborative; students work with peers and, in many authentic projects, also with adults from outside the classroom. Speaking clearly and persuasively and listening to others are vital skills for this work.

Figure 4.2—C3 Framework Dimension 2: Applying Disciplinary Concepts and Tools

College and Career Readiness ELA Standard	Civics Connection
These 10 standards include reading skills in four categories: ★ Key Ideas and Details ★ Craft and Structure ★ Integration of Knowledge and Ideas ★ Range of Reading and Level of Text Complexity	To gain knowledge for their inquiry, students will need to read a variety of texts, of a wide range of complexity. They will need to read closely for meaning; determine main ideas, details, structure, purpose, source type, and claims from the sources; and compare multiple sources.

Figure 4.3—*C3 Framework Dimension 3: Evaluating Sources and Using Evidence*

College and Career Readiness ELA Standard	Civics Connection
Gather relevant information from multiple print and digital sources, assess the credibility and accuracy of each source, and integrate the information while avoiding plagiarism.	As part of their inquiry process, students will be gathering information from a wide variety of sources, whose credibility and accuracy will need to be assessed.
Draw evidence from literary or informational texts to support analysis, reflection, and research.	When students develop their answers to the compelling questions that frame their inquiry, they will need to use evidence.

Figure 4.4—*C3 Framework Dimension 4: Communicating Conclusions and Taking Informed Action*

College and Career Readiness ELA Standard	Civics Connection
These 10 standards include writing skills in four categories: ★ Text Types and Purposes (includes arguments and informative/ explanatory texts) ★ Production and Distribution of Writing (includes using technology to produce and publish writing) ★ Research to Build and Present Knowledge ★ Range of Writing (includes "time for research, reflection, and revision")	At the end of their inquiry, students communicate their answers to their questions in writing (when they are old enough). This will take the form of an argument/opinion piece and/or an informational/explanatory piece. In many authentic activities and projects, students will publish their work for an audience beyond the classroom. Their work will undergo rounds of critique and revision.

College and Career Readiness ELA Standard	Civics Connection
Presentation of Knowledge and Ideas: ★ Present information, findings, and supporting evidence such that listeners can follow the line of reasoning and the organization, development, and style are appropriate to task, purpose, and audience. ★ Make strategic use of digital media and visual displays of data to express information and enhance understanding of presentations. ★ Adapt speech to a variety of contexts and communicative tasks, demonstrating command of formal English when indicated or appropriate.	When students share their conclusions with others, and especially when they take action on civic issues and problems, they will need to present ideas effectively. Civic participation requires the use of reason and evidence when discussing issues or trying to persuade others. In many activities and projects, students will create digital media and visual displays. They will also need to speak to a variety of people, for a variety of purposes.

Connecting Civics and Literacy

Teaching civics enhances a school's literacy program because it creates an authentic purpose for literacy instruction. When students are learning civics by engaging with compelling questions, they have a meaningful reason to read and write. Civic education increases content knowledge for students, which improves reading comprehension (Tyner and Kabourek 2020). Civic education includes informational texts, which are important for meeting English language arts standards. It also creates opportunities for addressing speaking and listening standards.

Every elementary school has a literacy program. Some develop their own or use a mix of their own materials and commercially available programs. Most public elementary schools use a district- or state-adopted literacy model. Some of these must be followed with strict fidelity, while others are more flexible and allow for some adaptations and additions. You can connect your program to civics no matter what kind of program you have.

Elementary Teachers

If you're an elementary teacher and your school uses a literacy program that is somewhat flexible, you can incorporate civics relatively easily:

★ Use fiction and nonfiction texts that connect to civics lessons and projects for guided reading. An exciting new resource is *iCivics Readers*, a K–5 series from Teacher Created Materials (**tcmpub.com**). This resource provides leveled, high-interest texts and lesson plans that teach students the ins and outs of civic education.

★ Use read-alouds that connect to civics units and projects.

★ Have students work on writing assignments for civics lessons and projects during a writers' workshop.

★ Connect "working with words" or academic vocabulary words to civics lessons and projects.

★ Connect literature circles and book club texts to civics lessons and projects.

If your school uses a literacy program that is not flexible, civics lessons and projects will probably need to be taught separately, but you can still connect the two subjects. When engaged in civics, help your students see the connections:

★ Remind students of the literacy strategies taught during your English language arts instruction, and have them apply those strategies when reading for civics lessons and projects.

★ Use the same scaffolding strategies for writing when students write in civics lessons and projects.

★ Use literature circles or book clubs for reading and discussing texts in civics lessons and projects.

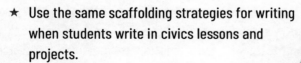

Secondary Teachers

If you are a secondary teacher and teach social studies, you are probably expected to also teach literacy skills. However, you likely are not required to adhere to a strict literacy program, which gives you some flexibility. You can do many of the same things we recommend for elementary teachers to connect literacy and civics:

★ Think about literary practices that are core to civics and history: How can someone read and make sense of a government document, a court ruling, or a candidate's website? How can we comprehend the meaning of something written over 200 years ago, such as the Declaration of Independence or the Constitution? An excellent free resource is *Reading Like a Historian*, a K–12 inquiry-based curriculum from the Stanford History Education Group (**sheg.stanford.edu/ history-lessons**).

★ Incorporate challenging primary sources, from historical and legal documents to informational text to voter materials. These can be difficult for adult readers, so they may require extra scaffolding for older students. We recommend "Tampering with History: Adapting Primary Sources for Struggling Readers" at the National Council for the Social Studies (**www.socialstudies.org/social-education/73/5/ tampering-history-adapting-primary-sources-struggling-readers**) and Primary Source Sets from the Digital Public Library of America (**dp.la/primary-source-sets**).

★ When students are creating authentic written products in a civics project that are meant to replicate real-world writing, show them "mentor texts," or exemplars of what is expected to help them understand the type of writing required.

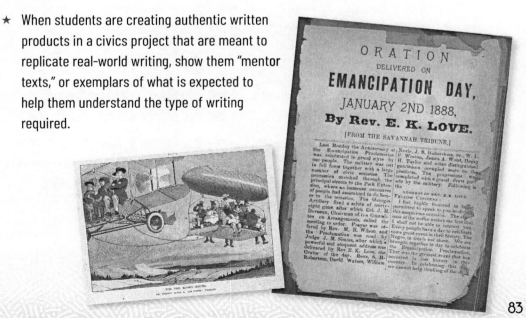

Integrating Civics into Literacy Instruction

Elementary teachers often say they don't have time to teach social studies, in general, and civics, specifically. It is quite easy, however, to teach civics during your English language arts program with the use of carefully selected texts:

* Choose texts at appropriate reading levels. For younger children, look for phonics skills addressed in the text. Teach corresponding phonics lessons, and refer to the text to show the application of the letters and sounds.

* Identify academic vocabulary that might confuse students. Teach word meaning, and show how context can be useful in determining the meanings of words.

* Look for ways to use the text to teach fluency. Have students practice reading passages aloud smoothly and accurately. Teach them how to read aloud with appropriate phrasing and expression.

* Determine ways to build comprehension using tools such as graphic organizers, monitoring comprehension, asking and answering questions, drawing conclusions, making predictions, identifying cause-and-effect relationships, and summarizing.

* For older students, determine ways to have students extract and use information from the text.

When integrating civics into your literacy instruction, a strategic approach is most effective. One recommended model for working with texts is provided below.

Lesson Model

1. **Preview the text:** Have students preview the text, skimming through the pages to look at titles, subtitles, and visuals, such as photos, charts, and graphs.

2. **Make predictions:** Ask students to make predictions about the text. "What is it about?" "What will we learn from it?" "How might we be able to use the information to make a difference and make positive changes in the community?"

3. **Mark the text:** Provide students with sticky notes. As they read, encourage them to write comments, questions, personal experiences, or areas of confusion on the sticky notes, attaching them near the text that inspired their thoughts. After reading, have students refer to their comments, and engage them in a class discussion.

4. **Ask questions:** Encourage students to ask lots of questions about the text. "Why did the author write this?" "What does the author hope we will do with this information?" Model a think-aloud strategy as you turn your thoughts and wonderings into clearly articulated questions.

5. **Reflect in writing:** Have students extend their reading experiences by reflecting in writing. Have them write their impressions of the topic and record new information they learned and areas of further curiosity.

Integrating Literacy into Civics Instruction

Skilled readers engage in a variety of practices when reading. They monitor their own comprehension, ask and answer their own questions, activate prior knowledge, make inferences, draw conclusions, and summarize information. A problem arises when teaching other subject areas when students have not developed such skills and are not able to extract meaning from challenging texts about complex topics. Romance and Vitale (2012) state that students need to be taught to set purposes for reading and use strategies to deeply understand complex informational texts. Those who don't, will struggle.

In addition to comprehension skills, students need to learn academic vocabulary to aid their understanding. In her book *Tools for Teaching Academic Vocabulary* (2014), Janet Allen emphasizes establishing certain practices in the classroom, such as providing rich language experiences, teaching individual words, teaching word-learning strategies, and encouraging students to engage with words. She also highlights the type of academic vocabulary that should be taught: general academic vocabulary, domain-specific vocabulary, topic-specific vocabulary, and passage-specific vocabulary. Academic vocabulary is the language of the discipline, and without it, students' comprehension will suffer.

Content-area teachers often report they do not have the time to teach literacy skills in their classes, but without these important skills, students will often not grasp the concepts. Not only that, but content-area literacy strategies should not be taught separately from content. "If you are doing it right, you should not have to take much (or any) extra time out of your instruction to teach content-area literacy skills" (McGlynn and Kelly 2018).

Students engage with a variety of texts in social studies classrooms, including primary and secondary sources. In addition to understanding content, they need to summarize and analyze information, as well as weigh evidence and develop arguments. Reading, writing, listening, and speaking are all natural ways to process and share civics content.

Strategies for Reading to Learn

Through these areas of literacy, students develop clear, more flexible thinking, which is essential when encountering topics in civics. You can integrate literacy into your civics curriculum with minimal effort.

Activate Prior Knowledge

When students make connections to texts, they have deeper levels of understanding. As you introduce a civics text, ask students what they know about the topic, and invite them to share personal stories or experiences related to it. If students struggle with this, model for them using a think-aloud strategy, where you share your personal experiences related to the topic.

Pre-Teach Vocabulary

Reading civics-related texts provides an excellent opportunity to develop academic vocabulary and clear up confusion over potentially confusing or unfamiliar words. Pre-teaching vocabulary increases student comprehension and reduces the complexity of the text as a whole. More specifically:

★ If academic vocabulary words are emphasized in bold text, ask students to locate the words. Otherwise, provide a list of words for students to find in the text.

★ Pronounce a new word aloud. Have students read the sentence or paragraph containing the new word and try to determine its meaning in context.

★ Provide each student with a four-column vocabulary chart. Ask them to write a vocabulary word in the first column. In the second column, have students write what they think the word means based on context. In the third column, students should write the actual definition of the word after class discussion or after looking up the meaning in a glossary or dictionary. In the final column, have students write an original sentence using the word.

Teach Academic Vocabulary

★ Teach general academic vocabulary, including how to analyze, synthesize, and define. These are not specific to a particular subject area.

★ Teach domain-specific vocabulary, or the words that are specific to a particular discipline.

★ Teach topic-specific vocabulary, which is a subset of domain-specific vocabulary and is more targeted at a specific topic.

★ Finally, teach passage-specific vocabulary. These are words that appear in the text that are not related to the topic but might confuse students and impede understanding of the passage if they don't know them.

Multiple Exposures to Vocabulary

To have deep understanding of vocabulary, it is important for students to have multiple exposures. Learning words one day and never addressing them again is not sufficient. Teach vocabulary by having students use it in speaking and writing, and demonstrating the use of vocabulary as you teach and speak.

Ask Questions

Skilled readers interact with texts. They think and ask questions about the texts they read. Inspire this interaction by encouraging students to ask questions about a text, including the illustrations and captions, before they begin reading. Encourage them to ask about any new vocabulary or anything they're curious about. Provide each student with a few sticky notes on which to write their questions. They should return to these questions after reading to see if they can answer them.

Set a Purpose for Reading

Set your own purpose for students' reading. Why are they reading this text? What do you want them to learn or discover? How do you want them to be inspired? Post a question or two on the board, and say, "As you read, look for the answers to _____ ." Setting a purpose for reading increases students' comprehension and engagement with the text far more than asking them to read a passage and then quizzing them at the end.

3-2-1 Strategy

As students read, tell them to find and write three facts, write two pieces of information that were confusing, and think of one question. After accomplishing this, have students meet in pairs or small groups to share what they wrote and attempt to clarify information and answer the questions they asked (ASCD 2017).

QAR (Question-Answer-Relationships)

Ask students to answer different kinds of questions that prompt them to use the text in other ways:

* ★ Ask questions with answers directly in the text. The question you ask points to information explicitly in the text.

* ★ Ask questions that require students to use information from different places in the text. Students combine information to form answers.

* ★ Ask questions based on text but also require connections to personal experiences.

* ★ Ask questions that require engagement with students' backgrounds and prior knowledge. For these answers, no text is needed.

Monitor Comprehension

We have all experienced reading without paying attention. Engaging with text and monitoring comprehension is an important skill that can be taught. Provide students with sticky notes for writing their questions. Encourage them to reread text that is not clear or to find answers to their questions. Ask them to think about their personal experiences with the topic. By having students actively engage with the text when reading, they will pay closer attention, be curious about the text, and seek deeper understanding.

Draw Conclusions

Encourage students to use information in the text to draw conclusions. When they state their conclusions, ask them to use facts and examples from the text to support them.

Make Inferences

Authors often make points that are implied, not explicitly stated. Having students make inferences is critical. Ask students first to identify the author's point. Then, have them find explicit examples of the author's point. Finally, have them state inferences based on what the author implied.

Summarize Information

Help students summarize what they read by having them address *who, what, when, where, why,* and *how* questions. After addressing each of the questions, have students write brief but thorough summaries of the text.

Inclusive Texts in Civics

You're probably already aware of the need to use books, stories, and other texts written by diverse authors in your teaching. It's important that students see reflections of themselves in what they read. If they don't, they're getting a message about whether they are valued—or are not—in our society.

Reading can also be a way for students to hear from and learn about people from backgrounds unlike their own, which supports the democratic value of taking the perspective of others. If you teach in a predominantly white community, it's important for students to see the literary contributions of people of color to help overcome stereotypes and deficit models. The same holds true, wherever you teach, for hearing the voices of underrepresented groups.

While textbook publishers and providers of curriculum materials have been catching on to the need, you may need to do some digging on your own to ensure the inclusion of diverse authors.

Strategies for Writing to Learn

Writing in the content areas means students learn writing as a routine. Students at all grade levels should be writing all throughout the day, every day. Think of it not as "ready, set, write" but more as a way of reflecting, recording evidence, making arguments, posing questions, and sharing information. Writing should be a natural extension of the learning process for several reasons:

- ★ to reflect on what was learned

- ★ to pose questions for further investigation

- ★ to document new understandings

- ★ to explain new concepts

- ★ to apply knowledge for solving problems

- ★ to share information with others

This section describes a number of ways to infuse civic instruction into writing.

Writing Fluency

Build writing fluency with short bursts of writing. Pose a civics topic or word related to the topic. Tell students to write as much as possible in one minute. When time is up, allow students to review what they wrote, briefly correcting any errors they notice. When students write in this way over the course of time, the amount they write and the depth of what they write will increase.

Shared Writing Experiences

Have students participate in shared writing experiences. Shared writing focuses on a specific purpose and involves a negotiation between teacher and students. It is also the perfect opportunity to model your thinking about writing, which serves as a model for students. As students participate in shared writing experiences more frequently, the process will become natural, and it will assist them in their own individual writing.

A Shared Writing Experience

Your students are learning about ways they can help their communities. Pose the questions: *In what ways can we help in our neighborhood and city? What benefits will our actions have on our community?* If a student offers an idea, write it on the board or on chart paper. Repeat what the student said and what is now written.

Think aloud to model your thought process. You could say, "I know it's a good idea to volunteer my time in my community, but I wonder about the long-term effects of that. I guess if other people see me volunteering, they might decide to do it as well. How could I add that thought to our writing?"

Write to Explain and Inform

Have students write to explain concepts or inform others about what they are learning. This is a natural extension of civic education, as a large part of civics is spreading the word about issues, getting others involved, and making a difference. Encourage students to clearly explain complex ideas in a way that others can understand.

Gather Information

Encourage students to gather information from sources. Facts can be written on note cards or infused into writing projects. Emphasize the use of citations without plagiarizing.

Write for Different Purposes

Have students write for different purposes. Students might write to share facts about what they have learned. They might write to persuade their friends and family members to take action. Each civics topic will lend itself to a particular writing purpose, so think about the kind of writing that best suits the topic.

Think of the Audience

As students write, have them think about the audience they want to inspire or persuade. Sharing information with a second grader requires a different style of writing than sharing with an adult.

Brainstorm Topics

Have each student create a list of possible writing ideas related to a particular civics topic. Ask students to answer "Why would I write about this?" and "What is the purpose?"

Cause and Effect

Civics topics usually have an impact on society, so it is easy to see cause-and-effect relationships. Have students brainstorm the causes of problems and the effects of change.

Predictions

Have students predict how something will turn out as a result of community action. What will change in the community, for example, if all citizens start to volunteer? Have students write their predictions so they can refer back to them later.

Persuasion

Ask students to reflect on and write about how they might persuade others to help make a change.

Compare and Contrast

Have students compare and contrast topics related to civics, such as political candidates or solutions to environmental issues. Thinking through issues in writing will help students reflect more deeply.

Class Encyclopedia

As students learn about a new topic, have them each contribute their knowledge to a class encyclopedia. This could be in paper form or on a class website.

Writing Fiction

Have students write fiction stories about civics topics. A student might choose to write a story about two friends who are learning how to be good citizens. Encourage students to show their knowledge of the civics topic by infusing facts into their fictional stories.

Strategies for Listening and Speaking to Learn

Listening and speaking strategies are as important as reading and writing. They help develop students' understandings of new concepts. They develop brand new concepts into formulated thoughts. As Terry Roberts and Laura Billings (2008) state, "Both speaking and listening are forms of thinking because they allow a nascent thought to be refined through conversation. The better a student's verbal communication skills the more quickly his or her thoughts about a complex topic gain clarity and coherence." Not only are listening and speaking important for sharing what students learn, but the process of listening and speaking also helps students gain deeper understandings.

Listening Skills

Why should educators focus on listening skills? People assume listening is a natural process, but that is not always the case. In fact, we often focus on what we want to say next, rather than listening to what was said. We think we understand what was said when we often do not. Students need to be taught and encouraged to listen purposefully, reflect back on what the speaker said, ask questions, and formulate responses that begin with the speaker's point before adding their own comments.

Several speaking and listening strategies can help students in your civics classroom:

Discussions

Depending on the age of your students, you may need to model how to hold a discussion. Explain to students that group members take turns speaking while others listen and then have a turn to comment on what was said. Discussion is not simply having each person state an unrelated thought. It's about interacting with others in the group and learning from one another.

Group Projects

There is no better way to encourage students to communicate with one another effectively than having them work on group projects. Younger students may need to have roles assigned (such as the leader, the recorder, and the questioner, depending on the project). Be sure to assign a project that requires participation from all group members in order to complete.

Consider the Audience

When students share what they have learned in short speeches, make sure they consider their audience. Speaking casually with bits of humor might be appropriate for some audiences, while speaking seriously and professionally might be more appropriate for others.

Evaluate the Speaker

Tell students to actively listen to presentations by providing speaker evaluation sheets. Each student responds to questions or prompts about the speaker, such as:

★ What was the speaker's main point?

★ What did I learn?

★ What questions do I still have?

★ The speak inspired me to ____.

★ Comments for the speaker

★ Use visuals.

When presenting aloud to an audience, encourage students to provide information visually by using various forms of media. A student might create a chart or show an image that relates to his or her topic.

Before You Speak

Teach students the motto, "Before you speak, ask or think." Tell students not to raise their hands to speak until they have thought of questions or comments for a designated amount of time. This encourages students to deepen their responses, taking time to reflect on what has already been said.

Think, Pair, Share

Pose a question or prompt when the goal is to get students to speak about what they have learned. Have students *think* about or write a response. Students then get into *pairs* or small groups to talk about their ideas. Finally, students *share* their thoughts in a larger group.

Most Convincing Argument

While listening to groups of students present information about a topic, instruct students listening to determine which group makes the most compelling argument. Which argument makes the most sense? Encourage students to take notes about their thoughts to reference for later discussions.

Debate the Issues

Have small groups of students debate opposing sides of an issue. Students begin by meeting in smaller groups to research a topic and plan their arguments. Encourage students to think about how the other group will debate the issue and come up with counterarguments. Have the two groups debate the issue in front of the rest of the class. Then, allow the audience to ask questions and decide which group had the most compelling argument.

Books about Civics

There are many books about civics, government, voting, civil rights, and various issues in American history. Here are a few favorites:

Books about Voting

★ *Grace for President* by Kelly DiPucchio; illustrated by LeUyen Pham
A girl decides she wants to become the first woman president and runs in her school's mock election. (grades 1–3)

★ *Lillian's Right to Vote: A Celebration of the Voting Rights Act of 1965* by Jonah Winter; illustrated by Shane W. Evans
A 100-year-old Black woman walks to her polling place and thinks back on her family history and the long struggle for voting rights. (grades 1–4)

★ *What Can a Citizen Do?* by Dave Eggers; illustrated by Shawn Harris
Children perform various acts of good citizenship that turn an island into a community. (grades K–3)

★ *The Voting Booth* by Brandy Colbert
This story of two teens who meet at the voting booth explores differing world views. (grades 7-12)

Books about Government and Laws

★ *There Ought to Be a Law: A Bright Day at the State Capitol* by Portia Bright Pittman and Calvin Mercer; illustrated by Harry Aveira
This fun, engaging, yet serious book explains how bills become laws. (grades 1–4)

★ *For Which We Stand: How Our Government Works and Why It Matters* by Jeff Foster; illustrated by Julie McLaughlin
This book explains how the government really works. (grades pre-K–2)

★ *The Constitution Decoded: A Guide to the Document That Shapes Our Nation* by Katie Kennedy; illustrated by Ben Kirchner
This book is an engaging, word-by-word explanation of the United States Constitution. (grades 4–8)

* *The Everything U.S. Constitution Book* by Ellen M. Kozak
  This book explores the history of the Constitution and shows how it guides lawmakers and judges. (grades 7-12)

Books about Community

* *Maybe Something Beautiful: How Art Transformed a Neighborhood* by F. Isabel Campoy and Theresa Howell; illustrated by Rafael López
  This book is based on the Urban Art Trail in San Diego, California. (grades pre-K–1)

* *What Is Given from the Heart* by Patricia C. McKissack; illustrated by April Harrison
  This is a story of compassion and what can happen when we give from the heart. (grades pre-K–3)

* *A World without Color* by John Amos, Dustin Warburton; illustrated by Lenny K.
  Using the career of John Amos as a model, this book focuses on kindness and empathy and working well with others. (grades 1–4)

* *The Giver* by Lois Lowry
  A young boy who lives in a world of conformity and contentment learns the secrets behind his community. (grades 5–9)

* *The Education of Margot Sanchez* by Marisa Kanter
  The main character is trying to find her place as she straddles the worlds of her family, school, and community. (grades 7-12)

More to Come!

In this chapter, we considered integration of civics into a literacy program as well as integrating literacy into civic education. Any reading or writing lesson taught with an ELA or other text can be taught in the same way with a civics-related text. In the same way, skills that students would normally learn and use during reading and writing instruction can be infused into civic education. You simply need to think strategically in order to seamlessly interweave the informational texts with the skills. Now, let's move on to our last chapter, where we offer ideas and resources for teaching civics in your classroom and beyond.

Reflect and Apply

1. Is your teaching situation flexible? What challenges might you face with integrating civics into your reading/writing program?

2. What are some potential consequences of not teaching literacy skills during civic education? Have you noticed issues with this in the past?

3. Think of a civics topic you would like to teach in the near future. What are some of the reading, writing, listening, and speaking strategies you could infuse into your civics instruction?

Chapter 5

Civic Education in the Classroom (and Beyond)

As we've said in earlier chapters, there is a partisan debate about what civic education should be. Building on Westheimer and Kahne's categorization of citizens noted in Chapter 2, we see that some people tend to emphasize how our government works and knowing our democracy's founding ideals, documents, and major figures in history. They often say that instilling patriotism should be a goal. Others tend to emphasize civic action, believing that knowledge of government and democracy will be gained in a deeper way. They also believe students should examine where our nation has fallen short and argue that patriotism should not be blind loyalty but must be earned by becoming a nation more worthy of it.

We've suggested a middle path that combines both of these approaches. By advocating for "reflective patriotism," it is possible to teach K–8 civics and history in a way that allows students to appreciate the ideals upon which American democracy rests and, just as with any other academic skill, gain a deeper understanding through opportunities to experience and practice civics. Students need a certain amount of factual knowledge, and the best way to teach that is through active learning methods that may include taking action but also other activities and approaches.

Accordingly, the ideas and resources we share in this chapter come from a variety of sources across the political spectrum. Many of the materials and lessons are what were once considered "neutral" but today could be challenged from either side of the political divide. We will leave it up to you as a teacher of civics to decide what approach to take and which resources to use in your classroom. There are many factors you'll need to consider, of course, including your own beliefs and your community context, plus your school, district, and state policies and standards. Note also that some of the materials here are not examples of active learning themselves but can be used to teach factual knowledge within an "active" lesson or a project.

Look at these three examples of teaching civics through active learning:

 ### 1. The Recess and Lunchtime Rules Project (Grade 1)

The first graders were engaged in a lively discussion; their teacher was facilitating as best he could. It was early in the school year, and the class was still learning how to share ideas and listen to one another. The children were talking about the kinds of things other students did during recess and lunchtime that bothered them or were unsafe. The teacher was adding their questions about the situation to a list on chart paper that was started two days before, when the school principal had visited the classroom.

The principal explained that kindergartners, being new to the campus, needed to learn how to be good members of the school community. She asked the first graders to help their younger peers understand the rules for recess and lunchtime behavior and why they are needed. She also invited the first graders to tell her if they thought any of the rules needed to be changed or if any new rules were needed.

Some of the students' questions after the visit were about rules: Why do we have them? Who makes them? How can they be changed? Others were about the project they were beginning: What's the best way to tell kindergartners about rules? Should we make a presentation, a picture book, signs and posters, or a video? Do we need to talk with the kindergarten teachers? Can the principal come back to work with us?

Soon, the class would be surveying students, teachers, and school staff and learning about who makes rules that govern a school—from the principal to the federal government. Then, they would decide on their recommendations, how best to present them, and finally how to share the rules with the school community.

 ### 2. The Community Stories Project (Grades 3–4)

The students were busy and noisy, but very focused, as they put finishing touches on the displays they were about to hang on the walls of the local library. The project was nearing the big finish. In a few days, the class was hosting an event for the community to show their work and

explain what they had learned. Among the guests would be people students had interviewed.

The project began a few weeks ago, when the teacher posted iconic photographs from American history on the classroom walls. Students did a silent "gallery walk" around the room, writing comments and questions on sticky notes they put next to the photos. The class talked about what made the images powerful and what questions they raised.

The next day, the class took a trip to the local library to look at historical photos of their community from its archive. There, the teacher and the librarian explained the project: find stories about the community and explore its history, documented with one photograph and in writing, to share at a public event at the library. Students asked many questions, which were recorded on a shared Google document.

Along the way, students learned about what it means to be a member of a community, who shaped theirs and continues to, and how its history connects with larger events in the state, nation, and world. Working in teams of three, the students identified community members to interview. Before they went out to take pictures to go along with what they learned from their interviews, students were coached by a professional photographer, who told them about lighting and composition and gave other tips. The teacher taught them how to write short informational pieces to accompany their photos.

The class planned the event at the library and invited guests, including community members and families. On that day, students made presentations to reflect on what they had learned, and the guests walked around to look at their photos, read their writing, ask questions, and celebrate the students' work.

 ### 3. The Broken Laws Project (Grades 6–12)

Their teacher was impressed by how dressed up the students were. They were about to speak at a city council meeting, and they were nervous but excited. They were also confident; they had spent weeks researching the issue of curfew laws governing young people, so they knew their arguments for changing the law were solid and backed by evidence. Their parents and many other community members, some of whom the students had interviewed during the project, were in the audience.

This team had also had a dress rehearsal the previous week. Along with all the other teams in their class, they shared their ideas for either changing a law or proposing a new one in a community forum at their school.

Other teams focused on other issues, from environmental protection laws to first amendment rights. Each had developed a proposal for a new law. Most of them had chosen to share their recommendations in writing, in the form of a letter to an officeholder, a government agency, or an organization that worked to address the issue. One team wrote a series of opinion pieces published in a local newspaper. Another created a petition to put a proposal for a new law on the state ballot, with a campaign to convince voters to support it.

All the teams had learned a lot since the project began, when their teacher shared several examples of new laws or proposals in various states and cities that could impact young people. The class studied laws from American history that had affected certain groups in society. Students reviewed their knowledge of the levels of government and the legislative process, with an eye toward what pathway might work best for certain kinds of issues. They engaged in civic discourse at several points along the way.

When the city council reacted positively and agreed to carefully consider their proposal and the people and organizations replied to their communications and noted the quality of their work, the students felt proud and empowered.

Find projects just like these, with details on how to teach them, in the project library at **www.pblworks.org**.

These three examples are full-blown project-based learning (PBL) units. You do not have to do a series of them all year long—though you certainly could—as there are many other active learning strategies you could put into the mix. In this chapter, we'll look at some of these strategies, plus some great places to get lessons, materials, and other resources for teaching civics. We'll also list some additional ideas for PBL projects and where to find more of them.

Practicing Democracy in the Classroom

In addition to teaching civics through lessons, projects, and other formal strategies, you can teach civics informally by using democratic practices in your classroom. In other words, don't just teach students *about* democracy, engage them *in* democracy as part of your classroom culture. This idea goes all the way back to John Dewey, who argued that passive learning, as opposed to the active learning we describe in this book, does not prepare students for life in a democracy. Stephanie Schroeder reports that according to the Institute for Democratic Education in America, "democratic education incorporates the 'values of meaningful participation, personal initiative, and equality and justice for all' into the classroom" (2017, para. 2).

The basic idea is to make your classroom more democratic—which might mean you have to give up some control, if that's what you're used to. How far you go toward a democratic classroom depends on many factors, from your own comfort level and skill in managing it to the age of your students. We don't have the space here to get into the full range of possibilities, so we'll explain a few strategies and encourage you to learn more.

You can model and teach democratic norms and practices from the very beginning of the school year. This can include everything from encouraging civil discourse, as we discussed earlier, to allowing students to deliberate and make decisions. Give them a voice in setting classroom norms, allow them to make choices about what issues and topics to study, and provide avenues for sharing their ideas and making their voices heard. It's also important to foster close relationships with your students, which not only allows you to get to know them well but is also essential for a democratic classroom.

Conduct regular class meetings where students can discuss ideas and make decisions, reinforcing democratic values such as taking the perspective of others, giving evidence, compromising, and respecting differences. If you teach young children, you can even model and teach democratic norms and practices during morning circle time.

You can use tech tools to help create a democratic classroom. Students can share ideas, ask questions, and give feedback—both to you and to one another—using Flipgrid, Padlet, Kialo, YO Teach!, or NowComment. Use online polls to collect students' opinions. Video conferencing platforms all come with polling features or use tech tools, such as Mentimeter and Poll Everywhere.

Setting Norms, aka Community Agreements

Whether they're called norms, expectations, ground rules, or community agreements, the basic idea is the same: it's a set of statements about how we treat one another and act in the classroom. We like to use the last term because "community agreements" captures what citizenship in a democracy involves. They differ from "rules," which are usually imposed and enforced by the teacher, school, or district in a top-down manner and are meant to keep order, rather than being shared and meant for productive collaboration.

You might already be establishing norms at the beginning of each school year, but think about how you can tweak the process so it promotes a democratic classroom culture.

It's important to co-create community agreements with students, not only because it gives them a sense of ownership. It also creates opportunities to learn how to engage in civil discourse, make compromises, and arrive at shared decisions. One such process is outlined here:

1. Have students do a short activity that is also a lot of fun in small groups of 3–4 students. Search for activities such as the "Spaghetti Challenge," the "Index Card Tower," and the "Chopstick Challenge" online.

2. Ask students to reflect on how they worked together. Ask what worked well and how they overcame any challenges.

3. Explain what community agreements are and why they are important, and invite students to help create them for the classroom.

4. Have students generate and discuss ideas in small groups before a whole-class discussion. Give students an example of an agreement if you think it will help get them started.

5. Have each group share their ideas, and then lead a process for finding commonalities, narrowing down the list, and reaching consensus. Four to six items is usually sufficient. Avoid the "majority vote" approach because it may lead those in the minority to have mixed feelings about following them.

6. Look for ways to word the list of agreements in ways that promote civic values, such as:

   ★ We respect one another.

   ★ We listen to one another.

   ★ We help one another.

   ★ We share ideas and explain our reasons.

   ★ We make decisions that everyone can support.

7. Post the agreements in a prominent place in the classroom, and refer to them often.

It is important to revisit the community agreements every few weeks or every month. Ask students to reflect on how well they are being followed. What are we doing well? What could we work on? Do we need to revise an agreement on our list or add a new one? Also, consider whether the same agreements work well for every occasion; for example, when students work in teams on a project, will they need to agree on some additional norms, or will the class-wide norms be sufficient?

Resources for a Democratic Classroom

★ "Building Community, Day by Day: Morning Meetings help students and teachers connect and start the day on a positive note" (Learning for Justice). **www.learningforjustice.org/classroom-resources/lessons/building-community-day-by-day**

★ "The Democratic Classroom" (Shmoop) **www.shmoop.com/teachers/classroom-management/students-classrooms/democratic-classroom.html**

★ "Democratic Classrooms" (Learning for Justice) **www.learningforjustice.org/professional-development/democratic-classrooms**

Class Discussions, Debates, and Deliberation

You can teach students what it means to engage in civil discourse—to listen well, speak clearly, be respectful, and support arguments with evidence from solid sources of information— when they engage in discussions, debates, and deliberations in the classroom. The community agreements you and students have established for the classroom may work well for these occasions, but more or different ones may also be needed. Use a similar process to the one outlined previously to generate student input and reach consensus. Specific agreements could include:

★ We will support our arguments with evidence.

★ We will use good/reliable sources of information to back up our ideas.

★ We will challenge ideas, not people personally.

★ We will make our points without using too much time.

You can also support students engaging in discussions, debate, and deliberation with scaffolds to help them improve; for example, provide a notetaking guide, and teach them how to listen and note key points someone else makes. Have students use timers when practicing for a debate or formal deliberation, to help them learn how to make points succinctly.

Try audio or video recording of practice sessions so students can listen to or watch them afterward to reflect on how they use their voices, hand gestures, body language, eye contact, and facial expressions. The "Fishbowl" strategy is another good scaffolding method; have some students model or practice a discussion or deliberation while the rest of the class observes, then debrief the experience to draw lessons from it.

To scaffold speaking skills and respectful discourse, use sentence starters, which you could put on a poster on the wall for students to refer to, such as:

★ "I have a different perspective."

★ "I see your point, and I have a different idea. What about _____?"

★ "Can you clarify what you're saying about _____?"

★ "Can you give an example of what you mean by _____?"

★ "Where did you get that information about _____?"

Resources for Discussions, Debates, and Deliberation

★ "Speaking Kindness in Democratic Classrooms" (grades 3–5, 6–8, 9–12): Lesson Plans for Creating Norms
www.learningforjustice.org/classroom-resources/lessons/speaking-kindness-in-democratic-classrooms

★ Kialo (grades 6–12): An online tool that teaches students how to structure and conduct discussions, debates, and deliberation
www.kialo-edu.com

Public Speaking

Public speaking is something you often see on lists of things people fear most. Having students write and deliver speeches to an audience, either live or online, can be a powerful strategy in your civic education toolkit. It combines many of the key features of active learning: students find a topic or issue they care about, investigate it, develop arguments based on evidence, and share their ideas publicly, with the goal of influencing other citizens. And if you get students used to it through careful scaffolding and lots of practice, it likely will not be such a scary experience.

You can help students with their public speaking:

★ Have students practice public speaking in low-stakes situations. Give students a fun, easy topic or issue to talk about, such as "Should students be allowed to bring their pets to school?" or "Should there be pizza for school lunch every day?" Ask them to move to a place in the room to indicate whether they are for it, against it, or have a mixed opinion. Have them write three sentences explaining their positions and then pair up to share their ideas aloud.

★ Write a rubric or list of criteria for a good speech with students. Show videos of speeches—many examples of which can be found online—or make one yourself, and have students use the criteria to evaluate it. You could also have fun making bad speeches as an example of what NOT to do.

★ Have students practice giving speeches in small groups for peer feedback. Or try a "speed dating" approach where students pair up, deliver a short speech to each other, then move down the line to form a new pair.

★ Find civics-related topics, or ask students to choose one, for a more formal speech to an audience. Spend plenty of time on the writing phase, and provide several practice sessions with feedback from you and peers.

★ Audiences for speeches could be classmates, but giving a speech at a school event or other public setting will make it a more powerful learning experience. Plus, persuading others is a form of civic action.

If you search online, you'll find many resources and lesson plans for teaching public speaking. We've listed just a few to help get you started.

Resources for Public Speaking

★ "Kid President" videos (YouTube has many examples)

★ Project Soapbox from Mikva Challenge (grades 6–12)
  mikvachallenge.org/our-work/programs/project-soapbox/

★ "8 Fun Ways to Teach Public Speaking to Kids"
   kidadl.com/articles/fun-ways-to-teach-public-speaking-to-kids

★ Teacher Off Duty: "How to Teach Students to Own That Speech" (grades 6–12)
   teacheroffduty.com/teach-students-to-own-that-speech

Content-Focused Lessons and Short Activities

There are hundreds of sources for civics content and how to teach it, maybe more. Your school or district may also have civics materials from curriculum providers. The trick is to find the right stuff without overwhelming yourself.

When looking through civic education materials, use the same skills for verifying the quality that we recommend teaching your students: check where it comes from, who's behind it, who funds it, and so on. Some are clearly coming from biased sources. They may still be useful, but be aware of and intentional about using them. Other materials may be less obviously partisan but still reveal a particular agenda if you dig deeper and use your critical-thinking skills. Before you go down too many rabbit holes in a search of civics lessons or materials, we suggest a few places to start that are reputable and have a proven track record.

Resources for Civics Content Materials

★ iCivics (**icivics.org**)

★ Teacher Created Materials (**www.tcmpub.com**)

★ National Consitution Center (**constitutioncenter.org/learn/educational-resources**)

★ Constitutional Rights Foundation (**www.crf-usa.org**)

★ Bill of Rights Institute (**billofrightsinstitute.org/educators**)

★ Learning for Justice (**www.learningforjustice.org/classroom-resources**)

★ Smithsonian (**www.si.edu/educators**)

In addition to the providers listed above, Common Sense Media provides reviews of "Best Government and Civics Websites and Games" at **www.commonsense.org/education/top-picks/best-government-and-civics-websites-and-games**.

Simulations and Experiential Learning Programs

According to a recent report, teachers should "encourage students' participation in simulations of democratic processes and procedures. Evidence indicates that simulations of voting, trials, legislative deliberation, and diplomacy in schools can lead to heightened political knowledge and interest" (Gould et al. 2011). Simulations, including video games, allow students to learn by experiencing important civic activities that are not available to them in the real world. For example, a fifth-grade student could vote in a local election, a seventh grader could run for president of the United States, and a sophomore in high school could be a Supreme Court justice. Such experiences deepen student knowledge and even inspire civic dispositions. Civics is largely about process and motivation, and that is why simulations are so valuable. The applicability of civics in a virtual world empowers the learner to take steps in the real world. There are many resources to help you bring a simulation to life in your own classroom.

Resources for Simulations

Elections

★ Mock Election (iCivics)
  www.icivics.org/teachers/lesson-plans/mock-election

★ Voting—Learning How to Vote (ShareMyLesson)
  sharemylesson.com/teaching-resource/voting-learn-how-vote-267622

★ Hold a Mock Presidential Election (Scholastic)
  www.scholastic.com/teachers/lesson-plans/teaching-content/hold-mock-presidential-election

Legislature/Congress

★ "Lawcraft" game (iCivics)
  www.icivics.org/games/lawcraft

Courts

★ "Court Quest" game (iCivics)
  www.icivics.org/games/court-quest

Constitutional History

★ "The Constitutional Powers of Congress" (Bill of Rights Institute)
  billofrightsinstitute.org/lessons/constitutional-powers-congress

Citizenship

- ★ "Civics! An American Musical" game (FableVision Games)
  www.fablevisiongames.com/game/civics

- ★ "Immigration Nation" game (iCivics)
  icivics.org/games/immigration-nation

Resources for Experiential Programs and Opportunities

- ★ "Beyond the Ballot" (Generation Citizen)
  www.gobeyondtheballot.org/civic-action-toolkit.html

- ★ "Letters to the President" (Ronald Reagan Presidential Foundation & Institute)
  **www.reaganfoundation.org/education/curriculum-and-resources/curriculum/
  letters-to-the-president/**

- ★ Issues to Action; Project Soapbox; Student Voice Committee; Elections in Action;
  Creating Democratic Classrooms (Mikva Challenge)
  mikvachallenge.org/curricula/

- ★ "Project Citizen" (Center for Civic Education)
  www.civiced.org/project-citizen/program

- ★ "Action Civics and Experiential Learning" (Teaching for Democracy Alliance)
  www.teachingfordemocracy.org/action-civics-and-experiential-learning.html

Discussing Current Events

Bringing current events into civic education is a good idea. You'll need to manage it well to keep it engaging. It can also be tricky in today's political climate, but we encourage you to incorporate it in your classroom if you can.

Top 10 Reasons to Include Current Events in Civic Education

1. It helps students develop knowledge, skills, and dispositions for democratic citizenship.

2. It engages students by connecting abstract civics concepts with what's happening in the real world.

3. It makes students more likely to pay attention to the news and become informed, active, voting citizens.

4. It builds background knowledge, making it easier to form connections to new information.

5. It teaches students how to read informational text, including how to use features such as photos, captions, headlines, and subheads.

6. It promotes critical thinking by helping students learn how to ask questions, make inferences and predictions, and support their opinions with evidence.

7. It builds vocabulary and improves reading comprehension.

8. It can be empowering for young people by giving them the sense that they know what adults are often talking about.

9. It can make for interesting dinner table conversations at home and gives families opportunities to discuss their values.

10. It can be fun!

Adapted from Gould et al. (2011); Fletcher (n.d.).

The most challenging aspect of incorporating current events is managing the process well and maintaining objective learning goals, especially within today's polticized context. But with the right tools, current events can be a powerful learning tool in civic education.

Connect to Specific Learning Goals and Topics

Whether you bring current events into the classroom yourself or ask students to do it, make the process intentional. If you're teaching about the different levels of government, for example, find current events about actions taken by the city, county, state, and federal leaders, officials, and agencies. There could be a time when you want to allow students to find news stories about any topic they choose, but use that approach less often than a guided one.

Use Current Events to Teach Media Literacy

We discussed information literacy earlier, and media literacy is a valuable subset of that. Teach students how to understand informational text in news stories. Teach them how to look critically at what they read or see by asking questions such as who created something and what their purpose is, whether there is bias or a particular point of view behind the item, and whether it is based on fact or opinion. Ask "Is solid evidence given for an argument? How was this designed to get attention?" See the resources below for more on media literacy.

Have Discussions, Not Debates

This connects to our advice in Chapter 3 about how to handle controversial issues and how to engage in civil discourse. Debates often degenerate into activities that involve winners and losers, where scoring points is more important than arriving at informed opinions, shared understandings, and shared decision-making. Instead, engage students in a discussion. Media literacy scholar and educator Renee Hobbs suggests inviting students into discussion by asking, "What are all the things you have heard about this topic, regardless of whether you believe them or not?" (Ferlazzo 2020).

A discussion, Hobbs says, "invites general sharing and gathering of ideas, and it frees students up to offer ideas without being associated with or having to defend them. In this kind of activity, students can share information without isolating themselves from their group. Plus, this method does not alienate the students who aren't familiar with the news event or controversy under discussion. There's no penalty for not knowing. Students can learn about current events from their peers" (Ferlazzo 2020).

Resources for Discussing Current Events

Media Literacy

* ★ "10 Resources to Boost Student Media Literacy" (International Society for Technology in Education)
www.iste.org/explore/10-resources-boost-student-media-literacy

* ★ Media Education Lab
mediaeducationlab.com

* ★ Project Look Sharp (Ithaca College)
www.projectlooksharp.org/#

News Articles

* ★ Newsela (articles for differentiated reading levels)
newsela.com

* ★ Common Sense Media
www.commonsensemedia.org/lists/best-news-sources-for-kids

* ★ Yes! Magazine
www.yesmagazine.org/education

Ideas and Tips

* ★ "The Best Way to Teach Current Events? Let Students Lead." (KQED)
www.kqed.org/education/531646/the-best-way-to-teach-current-events-let-students-lead

* ★ "Current Events in Your Classroom: Teaching Resources for High School and Middle School Students" (Facing History & Ourselves)
www.facinghistory.org/educator-resources/current-events

* ★ "Teach Current Events as 'History in the Making'" (MiddleWeb)
www.middleweb.com/42919/teach-current-events-as-history-in-the-making/

Project-Based Learning

Project-based learning (PBL) is perfect for civic education. Students can learn in-depth about civics concepts, build the skills and develop the dispositions for citizenship, and investigate questions that are meaningful to them. Projects often take students out of the classroom to address real-world problems and issues in their communities and the wider world. There are a few stereotypes about PBL, however, that should be dispelled.

First, a project is not simply "making something." Think of some classic assignments that are often called "projects"—building a model of an Egyptian pyramid or an Iroquois village, making a poster of how a bill becomes a law, or researching a historic figure and making a presentation. These kinds of assignments might serve a purpose, but "doing a project" is not project-based learning. In PBL, the project is more like a curriculum unit. The project is the framework for instruction, rather than something done alongside a traditionally taught unit. Students are introduced to the project at the beginning, and it creates the reason for learning the targeted content and skills.

Figure 5.1 provides a model for these rigorous, extended projects we're talking about, developed by the Buck Institute for Education.

Figure 5.1—*Gold Standard PBL: Seven Essential Project Design Elements*

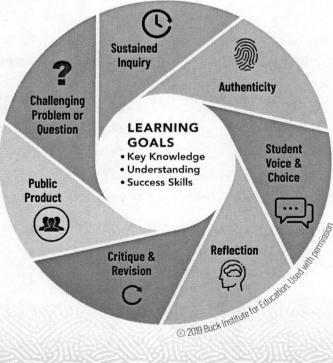

Second, the teacher plays an active role in planning and managing the project. Teachers don't step back and let students find resources to teach themselves. The teacher also still has a role to play in teaching the content and skills required to successfully complete the project.

Third, using PBL does not usually mean each student chooses a topic of interest and investigates it, then writes, creates, or presents something to show what they've learned. Most projects should be designed by the teacher (perhaps in collaboration with students) or designed by a curriculum developer. There's room for students to make choices within a project, but the whole class (perhaps divided into teams of students) works on it together. A PBL project has a structure, with four basic phases:

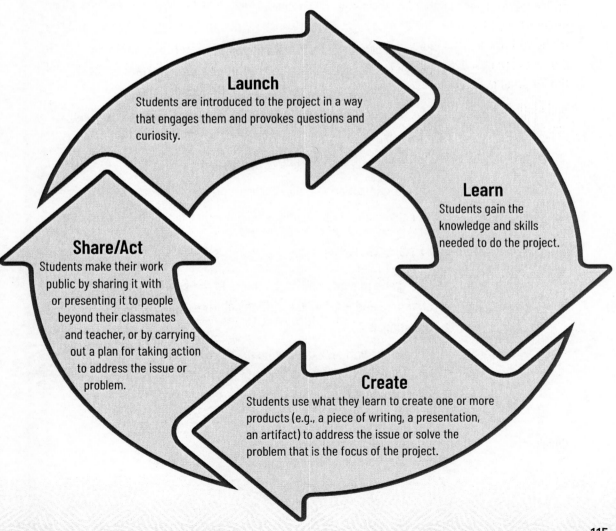

Launch
Students are introduced to the project in a way that engages them and provokes questions and curiosity.

Learn
Students gain the knowledge and skills needed to do the project.

Share/Act
Students make their work public by sharing it with or presenting it to people beyond their classmates and teacher, or by carrying out a plan for taking action to address the issue or problem.

Create
Students use what they learn to create one or more products (e.g., a piece of writing, a presentation, an artifact) to address the issue or solve the problem that is the focus of the project.

Find more information about how to design and implement PBL, plus project ideas and fully detailed projects, at **PBLWorks.org**.

The following section includes ideas for civic education projects in grade-level bands, many of which could be adapted for older or younger students. Some of these ideas are from specific sources. Others are simply ideas that you as the teacher would need to develop more fully.

Grades K–12 Civics Projects

This type of project could be used for students of all ages, adapted as necessary. Students identify a problem or issue in their school, community, or the wider world; research it; learn about ways to take action to address it; then make a plan and carry it out. Actions could include:

★ Deciding what level of government and which people have the power to do something about an issue, then writing letters to them. (See "Letters to the President" lessons at the Ronald Reagan Presidential Foundation.)

★ Creating a public awareness-raising campaign, using videos, posters, art, web pages, or social media.

★ Speaking with local government officials or at meetings.

★ Partnering with an organization to help address a problem or issue.

★ Making public speeches about an issue at a community event or online forum.

Grades K–2 Civics Projects

★ Students create a guide to share with newcomers to the school or community, with an illustrated map and written descriptions of important places (Buck Institute for Education, n.d.).

★ Students learn about the various people who make up or work in their community and plan an event to honor a particular group (e.g., small-business owners, farmers, seniors, health care workers).

★ Students think about what makes someone a hero, decide which people in their local community could be called a hero, then choose one to interview. They create portraits of their heroes and write captions, which are displayed in a public space with a grand opening event (Buck Institute for Education, n.d.).

★ Students create videos and a picture book with written captions about how to take care of their school campus environment, which they share with other students and school staff (Buck Institute for Education, n.d.).

★ Students study an issue such as hunger in their community, and decide on an action to take, such as collecting contributions to a food bank, raising money for an organization, or doing an awareness-raising campaign (Buck Institute for Education, n.d.).

★ Students interview people in their local area to create a community magazine with writing, pictures, and other features to show how different people and places contribute to what it means to be a community (Lim, n.d.).

Grades 3–5 Civics Projects

★ Students explore the question "Did the American Revolution have more than two sides?" and consider the perspectives of the Founders, the British and the French, colonial loyalists, enslaved people, Indigenous people, and others, and create multimedia to share their conclusions (Buck Institute for Education, n.d.).

★ Students plan and conduct an election in their school that reflects how local, state, and/or national elections are held (**www.icivics.org/teachers/lesson-plans/mock-election**).

★ Students create public works of art, such as a mural, sculpture, or performances, to commemorate their community's history, raise awareness of an issue, or honor people who have served their community.

★ Students learn about the Bill of Rights and what "liberty" means as they create comic books to teach others about their rights and freedoms in the United States.

★ Students create podcasts by interviewing a variety of people about what freedom in America means to them and reflecting on what they learned.

Grades 6–12 Civics Projects

★ Students learn how to determine the quality of a source of information that citizens might use to make decisions about civics-related issues or candidates for office. They then conduct an awareness-raising campaign for other students, families, and the community.

★ Students look at the mathematics of voting and weigh the pros and cons of various methods, such as 51 percent majority rule, ranked choice, plurality, and proportional representation, then decide whether they favor changing the methods. They express their opinions in letters written to government officials or the media (Buck Institute for Education, n.d.).

★ Students, with help from teachers and families, are partnered with a first-generation immigrant, if possible someone from a different ethnic background and not a relative. Through research on the person's home country and a series of interviews, students learn why people emigrate and what it means to "become American." Students commemorate the person by creating an artistic or multimedia product for a public exhibition night (Abbassi and Ganesan, n.d.).

★ Students investigate the history and meaning of the Pledge of Allegiance, consider questions of ideals vs. reality, how they feel about it, and whether all students should be required to say it. They express their thoughts in a persuasive essay for publication.

★ Students create videos to share on YouTube, TikTok, or other social media platforms to demonstrate what "civil discourse" is and is not and why it's important. They roleplay scenes of people engaged in deliberation vs. debate, arguing a position with and without good evidence, civil discourse vs. uncivil communication, and so on.

★ Students consider the question "Should voting be mandatory?" and examine how this approach works in other countries. They communicate their conclusions in written opinion pieces or letters to election officials or other government representatives.

In Conclusion

We've given you a lot to ponder. We hope it whetted your appetite for teaching civics and gave you the nourishment you need. Or if you already are a dedicated teacher of civic education, we hope you gathered some new ideas, strategies, and resources. There is much more we could have said, since civic education is such an important topic, especially in these times in our country. It's also an ever-evolving topic, so we know there will always be new things to learn and consider. It's going to stay in the news, we think, for a long time.

We said it before, and we'll say it again: you have an important job to do. Our democracy needs you. May you teach our children well.

Reflect and Apply

1. Consider the challenges of creating a democratic classroom. How could you best overcome those challenges?

2. Do you use debates in your classroom? What might be one challenge in transitioning from a culture of debates to one of discussions? How might you use civic education to help students understand the proper time and place for debate, as well as what civil debate looks like?

3. How might your students benefit from project-based learning? Of the projects listed, which would be most beneficial for your students and their learning?

References

Abbassi, Leily, and Jennie Ganesan. n.d. "The New Americans Project." *High Tech High*. Accessed July 15, 2021. www.hightechhigh.org/htm/project/new-americans-project.

Allen, Janet. 2014. *Tools for Teaching Academic Vocabulary*. Portsmouth, NH: Stenhouse Publishers.

Anti-Defamation League. n.d. "Moving from Safe Classrooms to Brave Classrooms." Accessed July 15, 2021. www.adl.org/education/resources/tools-and-strategies /moving-from-safe-classrooms-to-brave-classrooms.

Arao, Brian, and Kristi Clemens. 2013. "From Safe Spaces to Brave Spaces: A New Way to Frame Dialogue Around Diversity and Social Justice." In *The Art of Effective Facilitation: Reflections From Social Justice Educators*, edited by Lisa M. Landreman. Sterling, VA: Stylus Publishing.

ASCD. "Tell Me about How You Teach Content-Area Literacy." 2017. *Educational Leadership*, February 1, 2017. www.ascd.org/el/articles/how-you-teach-content-area-literacy.

Buck Institute for Education. n.d. *MyPBLWorks*. Accessed July 15, 2021. my.pblworks.org.

Cabell, Sonia Q., and HyeJin Hwang. 2020. "Building Content Knowledge to Boost Comprehension in the Primary Grades." *Reading Research Quarterly* 55 (51): S99–S107.

Center for Teaching Innovation, Cornell University. n.d. "Active Learning." Accessed July 15, 2021. teaching.cornell.edu/teaching-resources/engaging-students/active-learning.

Charles Koch Institute. 2018. "Why Is Civil Discourse Important?" charleskochinstitute.org /stories/why-is-civil-discourse-important.

Chauvin, Ramona, and Kathleen Theodore. 2015. "Teaching Content-Area Literacy and Disciplinary Literacy." *SEDL Insights* 3 (1): 1–10.

Chu, Dale. 2021. "What the Capitol Riot Means for Civics Education." *Flypaper*, January 21, 2021. fordhaminstitute.org/national/commentary/what-capitol-riot-means-civics -education.

Collaborative for Academic, Social, and Emotional Learning (CASEL). 2020. "CASEL's SEL Framework: What Are the Core Competencies and Where Are They Promoted?" October 1, 2020. casel.org/casel-sel-framework-11-2020/.

Eccles, Jacquelynne S., Bonnie L. Barber, Margaret Stone, and James Hunt. 2003. "Extracurricular Activities and Adolescent Development." *Journal of Social Issues* 59 (4): 865–889.

Educating for American Democracy (EAD). 2021a. "Excellence in History and Civics for All Learners." *iCivics*, March 2, 2021. www.educatingforamericandemocracy.org.

Educating for American Democracy (EAD). 2021b. "Pedagogy Companion to the EAD Roadmap." *iCivics*, March 2, 2021. www.educatingforamericandemocracy.org/wp -content/uploads/2021/02/Pedagogy-Companion-to-the-EAD-Roadmap.pdf.

Educating for American Democracy (EAD). 2021c. "The Roadmap to Educating for American Democracy." *iCivics*, March 2, 2021. www.educatingforamericandemocracy.org/the -roadmap/.

Ferlazzo, Larry. 2020. "Seven Ways to Bring Current Events Into the Classroom." *Education Week*, January 26, 2020. www.edweek.org/teaching-learning/opinion-seven-ways-to -bring-current-events-into-the-classroom/2020/01.

Fletcher, Lisa Marie. n.d. "Why Kids Should Study Current Events." *The Canadian Homeschooler*. Accessed July 15, 2021. thecanadianhomeschooler.com/why-kids -should-study-current-events.

Foa, Roberto Stefan, Andrew Klassen, Daniella Wenger, Alex Rand, and Michael Slade. 2020. *Youth and Satisfaction with Democracy: Reversing the Democratic Disconnect?* Cambridge, UK: Centre for the Future of Democracy.

Gould, Jonathan, Kathleen Hall Jamieson, Peter Levine, Ted McConnell, and David B. Smith, eds. 2011. *Guardian of Democracy: The Civic Mission of Schools*. Philadelphia: Leonore Annenberg Institute for Civics of the Annenberg Public Policy Center at the University of Pennsylvania.

Hansen, Michael, Diana Quintero, and Alejandro Vazquez-Martinez. 2020. "Latest NAEP Results Show American Students Continue to Underperform on Civics." *Brown Center Chalkboard*, April 27, 2020. www.brookings.edu/blog/brown-center- chalkboard/2020/04/27/latest-naep-results-show-american-students-continue-to- underperform-on-civics/.

Hatch, Orrin. 2017. "I Am Re-Committing to Civility." *Time*, June 17, 2017.

Health, Education, Labor and Pension, and Christopher A. Coons. 2021. *Civics Secures Democracy Act* §. 879 (117AD).

Hess, Diana E., and Paula McAvoy. 2014. *The Political Classroom: Evidence and Ethics in Democratic Education*. New York: Routledge.

Hoyer, Kathleen Mulvaney, and Dinah Sparks. 2017. *Instructional Time for Third- and Eighth-Graders in Public and Private Schools: School Year 2011–12*. Washington, DC: National Center for Education Statistics, Institute of Education Sciences, US Department of Education.

iCivics. 2020. *Why Do It? Teaching Controversial Issues*. www.icivics.org/sites/default/files/ field_collection/Why%20Do%20It%2C%20Teaching%20Controversial%20Issues%20 TG_0.pdf

Johnson, Elisabeth, and Evelyn Ramos. 2020. "Teach Current Events as 'History in the Making.'" *MiddleWeb*, May 12, 2020. www.middleweb.com/42919/teach-current-events -as-history-in-the-making.

Ladson-Billings, Gloria. 1994. *The Dreamkeepers*. San Francisco: Jossey-Bass.

Lepore, Jill. 2019. *This America: The Case for the Nation*. New York: W. W. Norton.

Levine, Peter, and Kei Kawashima-Ginsberg. 2017. "The Republic Is (Still) at Risk—and Civics Is Part of the Solution: A Briefing Paper for the Democracy at a Crossroads National Summit." Medford, MA: Jonathan M. Tisch College of Civic Life, Tufts University.

Levine, Peter. 2014. "What Should We Do?" *A Blog for Civic Renewal*, May 23, 2014. peterlevine.ws/?p=13846.

Levin-Goldberg, Jennifer. 2009. "Five Ways to Increase Civic Engagement." *Social Studies and the Young Learner* 22 (1): 15–18.

Levinson, Meira. 2010. "The Civic Empowerment Gap: Defining the Problem and Locating Solutions." In *Handbook of Research on Civic Engagement*, edited by Lonnie Sherrod, Judith Torney-Purta, and Constance A. Flanagan, 331–361. Hoboken, NJ: John Wiley & Sons.

Lim, Patricia. n.d. "First Grade Community Study and Magazine." *High Tech Elementary Explorer*. Accessed July 15, 2021. www.hightechhigh.org/htex/project/first-grade -community-study-magazine.

McGlynn, Kaitlyn, and Janey Kelly. 2018. "Science for All: Demystifying Reading in the Science Classroom." *Science Scope* 42 (3): 14–21.

The Nation's Report Card. n.d. *NAEP Report Card: Civics.* Accessed August 16, 2021. www.nationsreportcard.gov/civics/results/achievement.

National Center for Education Statistics. n.d. "Schools and Staffing Survey (SASS)." Accessed August 16, 2021. nces.ed.gov/surveys/sass.

National Council for the Social Studies (NCSS). 2013. *The College, Career, and Civic Life (C3) Framework for Social Studies State Standards: Guidance for Enhancing the Rigor of K–12 Civics, Economics, Geography, and History.* www.socialstudies.org/sites/default/ files/c3/C3-Framework-for-Social-Studies.pdf.

National Youth Leadership Council. 2008. "K–12 Service-Learning Standards for Quality Practice." cdn.ymaws.com/www.nylc.org/resource/resmgr/resources/lift/standards _document_mar2015up.pdf.

Packer, George. 2019. "When the Culture War Comes for the Kids." *The Atlantic*, October 2019. www.theatlantic.com/magazine/archive/2019/10/when-the-culture-war-comes- for-the-kids/596668.

Packer, George. 2021. "Can Civics Save America?" *The Atlantic*, May 15, 2021. www.theatlantic.com/ideas/archive/2021/05/civics-education-1619-crt/618894.

Putnam, Robert. 2001. *Bowling Alone: The Collapse and Revival of American Community.* New York: Touchstone.

Railey, Hunter, and Jan Brennan. 2016. *Companion Report: 50-State Comparison: Civic Education.* Denver, CO: Education Commission of the States. www.ecs.org /companion-report-50-state-comparison-civic-education.

Roberts, Terry, and Laura Billings. 2008. "Thinking Is Literacy, Literacy Thinking." *Educational Leadership* 54 (5): 32–36.

Romance, Nancy R., and Michael R. Vitale. 2012. "A Research-Based K–5 Interdisciplinary Instructional Model Linking Science and Literacy." *Science Educator* 21 (1): 1–11.

Sawchuk, Stephen, and Sarah Schwartz. 2021. "New National Civics Guidelines Carve a Middle Path for Teachers in a Polarized Climate." *Education Week*, March 1, 2021. www.edweek.org/teaching-learning/new-national-civics-guidelines-carve-a-middle-path-for-teachers-in-a-polarized-climate/2021/03.

Schroeder, Stephanie. 2017. "A Call for Democratic Education." *Learning for Justice*. Accessed July 15, 2021. www.learningforjustice.org/magazine/a-call-for-democratic -education.

Seibert, Daniel K., Roni Jo Draper, Daniel Barney, Paul Broomhead, Sirpa Grierson, Amy P. Jensen, Jennifer Nielson, Jeffery D. Nokes, Steven Shumway, and Jennifer Wimmer. 2016. "Characteristics of Literacy Instruction that Support Reform in Content Area Classrooms." *Journal of Adolescent & Adult Literacy* 80 (1): 25–33.

Shuster, Kate. n.d. "Civil Discourse in the Classroom." *Learning for Justice*. Accessed July 15, 2021. www.learningforjustice.org/magazine/publications/civil-discourse-in-the -classroom.

Smith, Julia, and Richard G. Niemi. 2001. "Learning History in School: The Impact of Coursework and Instructional Practice on Achievement." *Theory and Research in Social Education* 29: 18–42.

Smith, Steven B. 2021. *Reclaiming Patriotism in an Age of Extremes*. New Haven, CT: Yale University Press.

Stearns, Samantha. 2019. "'What Changed' in Social Studies Education." *Perspectives Daily*, July 30, 2019. www.historians.org/publications-and-directories/perspectives-on -history/summer-2019/what-changed-in-social-studies-education.

Stevenson, Bryan, and Sarah Lewis. 2018. "Truth and Reconciliation." *Aperture*, April 25, 2018. aperture.org/editorial/truth-reconciliation-bryan-stevenson-sarah-lewis.

Tocqueville, Alexis de. (1835) 2000. *Democracy in America*. Chicago: University of Chicago Press.

Tyner, Adam, and Sarah Kabourek. 2020. "Social Studies Instruction and Reading Comprehension: Evidence from the Early Childhood Longitudinal Study." *High Expectations*, September 24, 2020. fordhaminstitute.org/national/resources/social-studies-instruction-and-reading-comprehension.

Vinnakota, Raj. 2019. "From Civic Education to a Civic Learning Ecosystem: A Landscape Analysis and Case for Collaboration." *Red & Blue Works*. rbw.civic-learning.org/wp -content/uploads/2019/12/CE_online.pdf.

Westheimer, Joel, and Joseph Kahne. 2004. "What Kind of Citizen? The Politics of Educating for Democracy." *American Educational Research Journal* 41 (2): 237-2.